FROM SHADOW TO LIGHT

FROM SHADOW TO LIGHT

A JOURNEY OF SELF-DISCOVERY

MIGUEL ALMEIDA

CONTENTS

FOREWORD

Life is an intricate tapestry of experiences, each thread woven with wisdom, challenges, and revelations. Throughout our journey, many of us get lost amidst the noise of the world, forgetting the importance of truly knowing ourselves. This book is an invitation to all who wish to rediscover their essence, reconnect with the power that resides within them, and understand the purpose that brought us to this extraordinary planet.

Through the pages you are about to read, the author honestly and authentically shares his own journey of self-discovery. He leads us to reflect on profound questions: Who are we, really? Why are we here? And how can we access the infinite possibilities life offers us? With engaging and inspiring prose, he guides us to a deeper understanding of the cosmic consciousness that unites us all.

This book is not just a collection of reflections and teachings but a true journey of transformation. The author invites us to look within, to cultivate intuition, and to embrace the abundance that surrounds us. He reminds us that, regardless of the difficulties we face, we always have the ability to change our trajectory and create the life we desire.

Throughout the reading, you will find valuable insights and practices that can be applied in your daily life, helping you to awaken to your true nature and connect with the universe of possibilities around you. The central message is clear: The power to live an extraordinary life is already within you, and it is your choice to access it.

So, prepare to embark on this journey of self-discovery. May the words that follow inspire and guide you toward a deeper understanding of yourself and the world. May this book be a light on your path, helping you to discover the miracles that await you.

INTRODUCTION

From an early age, the search for self-knowledge and the understanding of our purpose on this extraordinary planet is one of the most essential lessons we can learn. In this book, I invite you to embark on a journey of self-discovery and transformation, where each page is an opportunity to reflect on who we truly are and why we are here. The extraordinary power that has been granted to us all — without exceptions — awaits to be revealed.

Like many, I was also a "victim" of the misinformation that permeates our society. I faced sadness, anguish, and disillusions, but I learned that everything that must be and happen, indeed happens. Resilience became a constant friend, guiding me in moments of uncertainty. At the age of 14, I made the bold decision to run away from home, a choice that led me to trust my intuition and the Cosmic Consciousness that connects us all.

In this world filled with abundance and possibilities, each of us has the power to create the life we desire. I deeply feel that my journey is a mission to share everything I have learned so that we can understand the magnitude of our potential.

Compared to the vastness of the universe's time, our brief existence is almost insignificant, but each of us is a winner in this marathon of life, a race that began long before our first breath.

It's crucial that we ask ourselves: What do we want to do with our lives? We are here, immersed in a temporary and illusory physical experience, and it's up to us to decide which experiences we wish to live. When reflecting on the movie of your life, what narrative would you like to watch? A story filled with adventures and achievements, or one filled with regrets?

Every choice we make shapes our destiny. Life is not a pre-written script; it is an open field of possibilities. Throughout this journey, I invite you to embrace the fullness of being and to ask yourself what brings joy to your heart. What can we do today that resonates within us and leaves a positive mark on the world?

Welcome to this journey of self-discovery and transformation. The path to understanding your true essence and the immense power that resides within you is about to be revealed. May your miracles begin to manifest through these pages, filled with cosmic knowledge and inspiration for an extraordinary life.

The Art of Repetition is the Only Path to Mastery

It is through repetition that we perfect mastery: we become masters. This is the essence of human learning, a truth that echoes through the centuries and is reflected in all areas of life. From the first steps when a child tries to balance, to the moment when an artist finds their unique voice in a symphony, repetition is the bridge that takes an amateur to a specialist.

In reading this book, you will notice that many themes are repeated throughout the chapters. Do not be alarmed by this; the intention is purposeful. Each time I revisit a concept, an idea, or a practice, I am inviting you to dive deeper, to explore nuances that may have gone unnoticed on the first reading. It is through repetition that we become masters of whatever we pursue.

Think about how you learned to ride a bike. The first attempt is full of falls and uncertainties. However, with each pedal stroke, you become more confident and skilled. The feeling of freedom that comes with mastery is the result of a continuous process of trial and error, of practice and repetition.

The same applies to any skill you wish to master, whether it's playing an instrument, cooking a recipe, or even developing healthy relationships.

REPETITION AS A GROWTH TOOL

We live in an era where speed and efficiency are valued, but, paradoxically, it is in the patience of repetition that we find true growth. The great masters of history, whether in martial arts, music, or literature, dedicated years of their lives to constant practice. They were not discouraged by difficulties or monotony; instead, they embraced repetition as a tool for growth.

Each repetition carries with it the promise of improvement. It's like sharpening a knife: with each pass over the sharpening stone, the blade becomes sharper and more effective. The same happens with our skills and knowledge. Every reading of a chapter, every practice of a technique, every reflection on a concept brings us closer to mastery.

The Awakening of Consciousness

It is important to emphasize that conscious repetition is

different from mere mechanical repetition. Repeating something without reflection can lead to stagnation, while intentional repetition, accompanied by self-assessment and the pursuit of improvement, leads us to a heightened state of consciousness. It is in this space of reflection that we find the greatest revelations about ourselves and our practices.

Therefore, as you advance in this book, I invite you to allow yourself to be a learner. Embrace repetition, not as a burden but as an opportunity for growth and development. Be open to revisiting concepts and practices, to exploring new ways of applying what you have learned.

The Legacy of Mastery

When we become masters of something, we not only enrich our lives, but we also have the opportunity to impact the lives of others. Mastery comes with the responsibility of sharing knowledge and experiences. As masters, we have the power to inspire, teach, and guide those who are on their own learning journey.

As you finish this book, I hope you take with you the message that repetition is a valid and powerful path. May you see each return to a theme as a chance to deepen your understanding and expand your skills. And, above all, remember that by becoming a master of something, you become not just an expert, but a beacon of inspiration for others.

In the end, true mastery does not reside merely in technical skill but in the ability to illuminate the path for others. By sharing your knowledge and experiences, you not only solidify your own understanding but also contribute to collective growth. Thus, repetition becomes not just a means of personal improvement but a legacy that extends beyond yourself. By embracing the art of repetition, you transform not only your life but also the lives of those around you, creating a lasting and meaningful impact on the world.

THE BALLOON OF THE COSMOS

If we look up at the sky, what can we see? The sky, right? But what does this vastness of blue or starry skies above us really mean? Imagine a balloon, a magical balloon, where this balloon represents the cosmos. Inside this balloon lies everything that exists, everything you can imagine.

Imagine the moon, a bright sphere that silently watches over us on the darkest nights. The sun, with its warmth and light, is the source of life that sustains and inspires us. The stars, with their constellations, tell stories of ancient times, myths, and dreams. The rainbow, a phenomenon that reminds us of the beauty that can emerge after a storm, and the celestial auroras, dancing in the sky in a spectacle of indescribable colors.

Within this cosmic balloon, we find the water flowing in rivers and seas, the trees rising toward the sky, the plants and flowers coloring the earth, and the humans who, in their search for meaning, look up in search of an answer. The birds slicing through the air, the mountains rising majestically, the cliffs challenging the sea waves—all are part of this great whole.

And we can't forget about the comets and asteroids, space travelers traversing the cosmos, reminding us of the vastness and mystery of the universe. The sand forming the beaches, the animals inhabiting the land and the air, the cars and planes taking us to new destinations, the fruits nourishing us, the bread and cheese gathering us around the table. Everything, absolutely everything, is part of this cosmic balloon.

And what's most fascinating? All of this, from the smallest leaf of a plant to the largest galaxy, comes from the same source, without exceptions. We call this source the cosmos, the creator of everything that has existed, exists, and will exist. The connection between each element within this balloon is deep and intricate, like the roots of a tree intertwining in the soil, forming an invisible network that sustains life.

As we allow ourselves to explore this idea, we begin to realize that we are not mere observers of this cosmos; we are part of it. Our actions, thoughts, and feelings reverberate through this vast balloon, impacting everything around us. Every smile we offer, every act of kindness, every gesture of love are like stars lighting up the darkness.

And if, indeed, everything is connected, then we must ask ourselves: how can we contribute to the harmony of this cosmos? How can we be the architects of a future where beauty and harmony prevail? The balloon of the cosmos invites us to dream, create, and act, reminding us that we are all part of the same universe, where each of us plays a vital role.

Thus, as we look to the sky, as we contemplate the balloon that harbors everything that exists, we are prompted to reflect on our place in this vast space. What stories do we want to tell? What legacies do we want to leave? The answer may be in the stars, but it's also within us, in the small actions of daily life, in the choices we make and the connections we establish.

In the end, the true magic of the cosmos lies in our ability to dream, to connect, and to create a world where everyone can shine together, like the stars illuminating the night.

May we always remember that, within the balloon of the cosmos, we are all interconnected and that our essence is part of a greater symphony, a cosmic dance that never ceases to amaze us. Each of us is a unique note in this universal melody, contributing with our own tone and rhythm, and together, we create a harmony that resonates through time and space.

As we walk this journey, it is vital to remember the power we hold in our hands and hearts. Our choices, no matter how small they seem, are like stones cast into a tranquil lake, creating ripples that extend beyond what we can see. An act of kindness can inspire another, an idea can spark a movement, and a dream can transform our world.

May we become agents of change, cultivating empathy and compassion in every interaction, recognizing that every being, every element of the cosmos, deserves respect and love. As we look to the sky, may we also look within, seeking our own light and the light of others, celebrating the diversity that enriches our experience.

With each sunrise, we have the opportunity to rewrite our story and the story of the cosmos. We can choose to be guardians of Earth, caring for nature and preserving the beauty surrounding us; we can be dreamers, those who dare to imagine a more just and enlightened future; we can be creators, those who express their art and ideas, making the world a more vibrant place full of life.

As we unite around greater purposes, recognizing our interconnection, we begin to perceive that the cosmos is not just a physical space, but an energetic space where intention and action interweave. Every day, in every moment, we have the chance to contribute to this great tapestry of existence.

As we look to the sky, let us remember that we are part of this cosmic balloon, and together, we can light stars and create constellations. May we inspire each other, share our dreams and aspirations, and work collectively for a future where harmony prevails, where every being can find their place and their shine.

Thus, as travelers in this immense cosmos, may we continue to explore, learn, and marvel at the infinite possibilities surrounding us. May our journey be marked by love, creativity, and the relentless pursuit of a world where everyone can thrive. After all, the true essence of the cosmos lies in our ability to dream and, together, make those dreams a reality.

At the end of each day, as we gaze at the stars shining in the sky, may we remember that even amid the vastness of the universe, we are never alone. We are interconnected, and each one of us is a precious part of the balloon of the cosmos, where the magic of life continues to unfold in all its glory.

UNIVERSE - THE BEGINNING OF EVERYTHING

(WHETHER WE LIKE IT OR NOT, EVERYTHING, ABSOLUTELY EVERYTHING, AND EVERY LIVING BEING ON THIS PLANET, IS THE COSMOS ITSELF. NO SEPARATION IS POSSIBLE.)

Once upon a time, in a time before time, there was an absolute and silent void, where there was no matter, energy, or even the concept of existence. This void was known as the Primordial Chaos. For countless ages, Chaos remained in a state of latency until, in a moment of pure possibility, something extraordinary happened: an infinitely small and dense singularity emerged from nothing.

This singularity contained all the energy and matter that would one day form the cosmos. Then, in an event known as the Great Crumble, the singularity exploded with unimaginable force, creating space and time and giving rise to the universe. This event was the Big Bang, a moment of pure creation that launched subatomic particles in all directions, commencing a cosmic dance that would last billions of years.

In the first moments after the Big Bang, the universe was a seething soup of elemental particles, quarks, and gluons, so hot and dense that no structure could form. But as the universe expanded, it also cooled, allowing quarks to combine to form protons and neutrons. These protons and neutrons, in turn, joined to form the first atomic nuclei.

Over hundreds of thousands of years, the universe's temperature dropped enough for electrons to be captured by these nuclei, forming the first atoms. Most of these atoms were hydrogen and helium. This process, known as recombination, released photons, which we can still observe today as the cosmic microwave background radiation, a kind of echo of the birth of the cosmos.

As the universe continued to expand and cool, gravitational forces began to act, causing hydrogen and helium clouds to condense into vast structures. Some of these clouds collapsed under their own gravity, forming the first stars. These stars, in their burning hearts, began forging heavier elements through nuclear fusion, elements that would be the building blocks for planets, moons, and eventually life.

The first clusters of stars formed the first galaxies, vast systems of stars, gas, and dust held together by gravity. Galaxies began grouping into superclusters, weaving the cosmic structure of the universe. In this cosmic tapestry, black holes, neutron stars, and an infinite variety of astronomical phenomena emerged, each more fascinating than the last.

Billions of years passed, and one of these galaxies, the Milky Way, witnessed the birth of a solar system in one of its spiral arms. Around a yellow star, eight planets and several smaller bodies began to orbit. The third planet from the star, Earth, possessed a unique combination of elements and conditions that allowed life to emerge.

Life on Earth began simply, as single-celled microorganisms, but over billions of years, it evolved into increasingly complex forms. Eventually, creatures capable of thinking, reflecting, and questioning their own existence arose. These creatures, humans, began looking at the night sky, amazed by the stars, and wondering about their origins. Thus, human curiosity led them to explore, discover, and understand the incredible journey of the cosmos from the Big Bang to the complex tapestry of life.

The story of the cosmos is a narrative of transformation and evolution, of order emerging from chaos, of simplicity giving way to complexity, and of a moment of creation that continues to unfold into a cosmic symphony that still fascinates and inspires us today.

The Stardust: A Philosophical Reflection on Origin and Destiny

The phrase "everything returns to its origin, to stardust" evokes a profound reflection on the nature of existence, the interconnectedness of the cosmos, and the inevitability of the cycle of life. These words remind us that everything we are, everything we know, and everything that exists in the universe has a cosmic origin, a history that dates back to the stars.

In scientific terms, the phrase refers to the reality that the elements that make up our bodies and the world around us were created in the nuclear reactions that occur in the stars. Hydrogen and helium atoms fuse under extreme pressure, forming heavier elements like carbon, oxygen, and iron. When these stars explode in supernovae, they scatter this "dust" throughout the cosmos, which eventually aggregates and forms new star systems, planets, and ultimately, life. Thus, we are literally made of stardust, a testament to the interconnectedness between all beings and the universe.

Philosophically, the idea that "everything returns to its origin" leads us to reflect on the cycle of life and death. In many spiritual and philosophical traditions, life is seen as a continuous cycle of birth, life, death, and rebirth. Each end is, therefore, a new beginning. Death, often viewed as a conclusion, can be reinterpreted as a transformation, where a being's essence returns to the cosmos, contributing to the emergence of new forms of life.

This cycle also applies to ideas and cultures. What we consider "ancient" or "past" is not lost; it transforms, reinvents, and returns in new forms. The influences of previous generations continue to shape the present and the future. Thus, the wisdom and learnings of the past are, in a way, the stardust that fertilizes the ground of what we are today.

Reflecting on the cosmic origin of matter also leads us to consider the interconnectedness of all things. If we all share a common origin, are we not, in essence, all part of the same cosmic fabric? This perspective offers a vision of unity and belonging that can transcend the superficial divisions of race, nationality, or belief. Understanding that we are made of the same stardust can promote greater empathy and compassion among human beings, encouraging us to care for one another and the planet.

The awareness of our stellar origin can also influence our perception of value and meaning. Often, in the rush of everyday life, we lose sight of the wonder of the simple act of existing. Every human being, every life, is a unique expression of the cosmos, a combination of experiences and stories that will never be repeated. Life, even in its fragility, is precious. Recognizing that we are part of something greater invites us to live more fully and meaningfully.

The phrase "everything returns to its origin, to stardust" is an invitation to a deep reflection on who we are and what our place is in the vast cosmos. It is a reminder that everything in life is cyclical and interconnected, that death is not an end but a transformation, and that each of us carries the essence of the stars in our being. By contemplating our cosmic origin, we can find meaning in life, in relationships, and in the continuous exploration of the universe. Ultimately, we are all travelers on the same journey, made of the same stardust, always returning to the origin that unites us.

Within this cosmic context, the quest for knowledge becomes a sacred activity. Science, philosophy, art, and spirituality are manifestations of our innate curiosity about the universe and our place in it. With each discovery, be it scientific or philosophical, we come closer to understanding the forces that shape our lives and the cosmos around us.

Scientists studying the stars, philosophers questioning the nature of reality, and artists expressing the beauty of existence are all, in a way, participating in this great cosmic dialogue. They help us realize that the quest for answers is, in fact, a quest for connection. Through knowledge, we can better understand not only ourselves but also the complexities and wonders of the universe.

With the awareness that we are made of stardust and that everything is interconnected comes a responsibility. The way we treat our planet, our communities, and one another reflects this understanding. If we are truly part of the same cosmic fabric, we must act in harmony with it, caring for the Earth and promoting peace and justice among beings.

The environmental crisis we currently face is a call to action. Recognizing that pollution, habitat destruction, and the unchecked exploitation of resources not only threaten our survival but also disrespect the common origin of all life. By taking care of the planet, we are, in fact, taking care of ourselves and future generations. The responsibility to preserve and protect our environment is an extension of our understanding that we are all part of the same stardust.

The phrase "everything returns to its origin, to stardust" also invites us to consider the transcendence of existence. If life is a cycle, and if everything we are and do is interconnected with a greater purpose, then our existence acquires a spiritual dimension. The search for meaning, connection with others, and the appreciation of life's beauty are ways in which we can transcend the banality of daily life and align with something greater.

Spiritual traditions around the world often speak about the quest for unity with the cosmos, self-realization, and integration with the whole. This quest can be understood as a way of returning to our origin, not just in a physical sense but also in a spiritual sense. Meditation, contemplation of nature, and practices that promote connection and inner peace are ways to reconnect with this cosmic essence.

Ultimately, the phrase "everything returns to its origin, to stardust" encapsulates a profound truth about life, death, interconnectedness, and the search for meaning. As we navigate our lives, we are reminded that we are part of a vast and intricate universe, made of elements that have once danced in the stars. May we honor this origin, cultivate the wisdom that emanates from it, and live in harmony with everything that surrounds us.

Thus, when we look at the night sky and contemplate the stars, may we not only see distant lights but also remember that we are made of the same matter as they are. And that, in every gesture of love, every act of care, and every search for understanding, we are, in fact, returning to our essence—the stardust that unites us all.

THE NATURE OF COSMIC CONSCIOUSNESS

Cosmic Consciousness is a concept that transcends the barriers of conventional understanding, challenging us to expand our perceptions of life, the universe, and our place within it. To comprehend its essence, one must first recognize that everything in the cosmos is interconnected. Like a vast ocean of energy and information, Cosmic Consciousness manifests in every particle, every being, and every phenomenon that composes reality. This interconnection is not just an abstract idea; it is a palpable experience that, when accessed, reveals the depth and complexity of life.

Imagine yourself sitting at the edge of a vast ocean. The water, in constant motion, represents the dynamics of Cosmic Consciousness, where each wave is a unique expression of energy and information. As you watch the waves rise and fall, you realize they are not isolated entities, but part of a larger system. The same is true of each of us: we are waves in this vast sea, interconnected by a vital force that transcends individuality. This force is Consciousness itself, a universal intelligence that permeates all forms of life.

Cosmic Consciousness is often described as a network of interdependence, where every human being, animal, plant, and element of nature plays a fundamental role. This network is not visible to the eyes, but can be felt in moments of profound connection, such as when we admire the beauty of a landscape or experience a moment of genuine love. In these instances, we are able to transcend the ego and connect with something much greater than ourselves. This connection teaches us that, despite appearances of separation, we are all part of the same cosmic fabric.

When we access this Cosmic Consciousness, we experience an expansion of perception. The limitations that normally imprison us—our beliefs, fears, and insecurities—begin to dissolve, allowing us to see reality in a new light. We come to understand that every thought and action reverberates in the universe, contributing to the web of life. This understanding is liberating and calls us to act with responsibility and compassion, recognizing that what we do to one affects all.

Cosmic Consciousness is also a source of wisdom that goes beyond intellectual knowledge. It manifests in intuitions, insights, and moments of clarity that often surprise us. When we tune into this universal intelligence, we are guided by a force that helps us make decisions aligned with our true purpose. This connection is not restricted to moments of meditation or spiritual practice; it can be accessed anywhere and at any time, as long as we are open to receiving it.

Moreover, Cosmic Consciousness invites us to explore the mystery of life. It is a reminder that amidst the complexity of the universe, there is an inherent simplicity that unites us. Each of us carries within us the spark of creation, a part of the whole that is uniquely expressed. This individuality is a celebration of the diversity that enriches our planet, allowing new ideas and experiences to flourish. As we connect with Cosmic Consciousness, we celebrate not only our uniqueness but also the beauty of the diversity that surrounds us.

As we delve deeper into the understanding of Cosmic Consciousness, we are invited to actively participate in this universal dance. Each of us has the power to shape reality, not only through our actions but also through our thoughts and feelings. When we align our intention with cosmic energy, we create waves of transformation that can impact the lives of others in unimaginable ways. This ability to influence the cosmos is one of the most powerful gifts we receive as conscious beings.

In short, Cosmic Consciousness is the vital force that connects us to everything that exists, a field of intelligence that invites us to transcend the limitations of the self and dive into the vastness of being. By accepting this connection, we find not only our essence but also the essence of the universe. We are all part of a vast ocean of energy and information, and by allowing ourselves to dive into this reality, we discover that true freedom and true power lie in the ability to connect and co-create with the whole. Thus, the journey to discover the nature of Cosmic Consciousness is not just a personal pursuit but a collective mission that unites us in the human experience. As each of us dedicates ourselves to this exploration, we contribute to an elevation of collective consciousness, an awakening that reverberates through the generations.

Cosmic Consciousness teaches us that we are all interconnected, and that each action, each thought, and each emotion has the power to impact the whole. Therefore, by recognizing and honoring this interconnection, we become agents of transformation, capable of creating a more harmonious and loving world. The true magic of life lies in our ability to unite, to celebrate diversity, and to co-create the reality we wish to see. Thus, by diving into the vast ocean of Cosmic Consciousness, we not only find ourselves but also become part of something infinitely greater—a continuous movement of love, light, and evolution.

THE DESTRUCTIVE POWER OF SELF-CRITICISM

Paths to Self-Compassion and Transformation

To break the harmful cycle of self-criticism, it is essential to cultivate self-compassion. Kristin Neff, in her research, proposes three fundamental components of self-compassion: self-kindness, a sense of shared humanity, and mindfulness. Self-kindness encourages us to treat ourselves with the same kindness we would offer a friend in difficulty. Instead of judging ourselves harshly, we must learn to recognize our flaws as part of the human experience.

A sense of shared humanity helps us understand that everyone faces challenges and struggles. This understanding can reduce the feeling of isolation that often accompanies self-criticism. By realizing that our difficulties are a common part of life, we can free ourselves from the pressure to be perfect. Mindfulness, in turn, teaches us to observe our thoughts and feelings without judgment, allowing us to accept our imperfections as part of the personal growth journey.

In addition to cultivating self-compassion individually, it is vital to create a positive environment around us. This can be done by promoting open dialogues about mental health and well-being, both at home and at work. Mutual support and encouragement for personal development are fundamental to reducing collective self-criticism. Organizations can adopt policies that value mental health, such as implementing well-being programs, interpersonal skills training, and safe spaces for emotional expression.

In educational environments, it is crucial to teach children and adolescents about the importance of self-compassion from an early age. Instead of focusing solely on results and performance, institutions should value the learning process, promoting a culture that celebrates effort and resilience. This prepares new generations to deal with life's challenges in a healthier and more compassionate way.

On a global level, the fight against self-criticism and its consequences requires a collective effort. Social networks, which often fuel comparison and dissatisfaction, can be transformed into platforms of support and encouragement. Campaigns that promote acceptance, diversity, and vulnerability can help change the narrative around perfection. By celebrating imperfections and stories of overcoming, we can create a space where everyone feels more accepted and valued.

Organizations and community leaders have a crucial role to play in promoting a culture of self-compassion and empathy. This includes creating initiatives that encourage volunteering, supporting vulnerable communities, and promoting dialogues about mental health. By emphasizing the importance of collective well-being, we can cultivate a more supportive and resilient society.

Self-criticism, while it can be a tool for growth, if not managed properly, can become a significant obstacle to quality of life, interpersonal relationships, and collective health. By adopting self-compassion and promoting an environment of support and empathy, we can not only improve our own life experience but also positively impact those around us and, ultimately, society as a whole.

Understanding that we are all human, imperfect, and constantly evolving is key to breaking the cycle of self-criticism. By doing so, we make room for a more compassionate world where vulnerability is seen as a strength, and our true essence can flourish. Thus, the journey toward transformation begins within each of us, resonating in waves that affect the lives of others and ultimately contributing to the construction of a more supportive and humane future.

THE TRANSFORMATIVE POWER OF CHALLENGES, IMPERFECTIONS, AND UNCERTAINTIES

In the intricate tapestry of life, challenges, imperfections, and uncertainties play fundamental roles that are often underestimated. Contemporary society, often obsessed with the pursuit of perfection and security, tends to marginalize these elements, treating them as obstacles to be avoided. However, instead of mere inconveniences, these factors are catalysts for personal transformation and growth.

How facing and embracing these aspects can not only enrich our lives but also make us more resilient and authentic.

Challenges are inevitable and, in many cases, are the driving force that pushes us out of our comfort zone. These obstacles can arise in various forms: unexpected changes in personal or professional life, health crises, natural disasters, or interpersonal conflicts. Each of these challenges brings with it a disguised opportunity. When we face a difficulty, we are forced to reevaluate our beliefs, priorities, and capabilities. This reevaluation often leads to an inner awakening, where we discover strengths we didn't even know we had.

A powerful example of this dynamic is the story of individuals who have overcome great adversities. People who have faced serious illnesses, significant losses, or financial crises often report that these experiences, while painful, were also moments of profound transformation. The act of battling a challenge can reveal resilience, empathy, and a new perspective on what truly matters in life. Ultimately, challenges teach us that even in difficulties, there is room for growth and renewal.

In the relentless pursuit of perfection, we often forget that imperfections are what make us human and authentic. Contemporary culture, fueled by social networks and often unattainable standards of beauty and success, promotes a distorted view of the ideal life. However, when we look more closely, we realize that imperfections are, in fact, the traits that connect us to each other.

Failures and mistakes are an integral part of learning. Making mistakes should not be seen as a sign of weakness but as an opportunity for growth. Each imperfection carries with it a lesson, as it forces us to reflect on our actions and reconsider our approaches. Furthermore, when we share our imperfections with others, we create a space of vulnerability that can strengthen interpersonal bonds. The authenticity that arises from accepting our mistakes can inspire those around us to do the same, creating a culture of acceptance and understanding.

Uncertainty is an inherent aspect of human experience. We live in a constantly changing world, where the future is unpredictable. This uncertainty can generate anxiety and fear, but it can also be a source of freedom and opportunity. When we accept uncertainty as a part of life, we make room for creativity and innovation.

Uncertainty forces us to be flexible and adaptable. Instead of clinging to rigid plans and forecasts, we can learn to navigate the turbulent waters of life with an open mind. This does not mean we should give up on our goals or dreams, but rather that we must be willing to alter our course when necessary. Many of humanity's greatest innovations and achievements have emerged in moments of uncertainty, when people were forced to think outside the box and explore new possibilities.

Furthermore, uncertainty teaches us to value the present. When we are aware that the future is uncertain, we are more likely to appreciate the moments we are living now. This awareness can lead to a fuller life, where every experience is valued, regardless of its final outcome.

When we put together challenges, imperfections, and uncertainty, we can observe a cycle of transformation that is intrinsically powerful. Challenges confront us with our limitations, imperfections remind us of our humanity, and uncertainty pushes us to live in the present. Together, these elements invite us to embrace a new narrative about what it means to live fully.

Personal transformation does not happen linearly; it is a process filled with highs and lows, moments of clarity and confusion. As we face challenges, accept our imperfections, and navigate uncertainties, we begin to perceive that each experience uniquely shapes us.

This journey teaches us that true strength lies in the ability to adapt and evolve, regardless of the circumstances. By embracing these aspects of life, we not only become more resilient but also more compassionate, both with ourselves and with others.

Therefore, instead of fearing challenges, imperfections, and uncertainties, we should welcome them as allies in our quest for a meaningful life. They are the elements that drive us to grow, learn, and connect more deeply with ourselves and the world around us. Thus, as we look to the future, may we remember that even amidst adversity, there is always the possibility of transformation and renewal.

INNER SILENCE AS A PORTAL

In the contemporary world, where distractions are many and incessant, finding a space of inner silence becomes an almost Herculean challenge. The noise of our lives, daily obligations, and the incessant notifications from our technological devices often alienate us from our true essence. However, as the French philosopher and writer Antoine de Saint-Exupéry wisely stated: "What is essential is invisible to the eye; one sees well only with the heart." This quote reminds us that true understanding and connection with Cosmic Consciousness cannot be perceived through external noise, but through inner quietude.

Cultivating inner silence is, therefore, an act of resistance and rediscovery. It is the portal that allows us to access deeper dimensions of life and connect with the essence of the universe. Meditation stands out as a powerful practice in this process, functioning as a bridge that links us to the vast sea of energy and information that surrounds us. When we allow ourselves to dedicate moments of our day to quiet the mind, we open a sacred space where Cosmic Consciousness can manifest freely.

Imagine yourself in a quiet place, away from distractions. You sit comfortably, close your eyes, and begin to concentrate on your breathing. At this moment, the wisdom of the poet Rainer Maria Rilke resonates: "The only journey is the journey within." Each breath becomes an opportunity to travel within yourself, to explore the unknown realms of your own consciousness. As you inhale, visualize that you are bringing the energy of the universe inside you. Feel this vibrant energy coursing through your body, expanding your awareness and illuminating your being. And as you exhale, release everything that no longer serves—fears, anxieties, and uncertainties—like leaves carried by the wind.

This process of silencing the mind and listening to the inner voice is essential for self-discovery and for connection with Cosmic Consciousness. Silence is not just the absence of sound but a fertile space where insights and intuitions can flourish. It is in this state of quietude that we can hear the wisdom that resides within us. The renowned thinker Eckhart Tolle said: "True liberation is liberation from thought." As we silence the mind, we begin to free ourselves from the limitations that have been imposed on us and access a new way of being—one that is in harmony with the whole.

As we delve deeper into this silence, we find a place of peace that transcends external circumstances. This is the space where Cosmic Consciousness reveals itself, where we become aware that we are part of something much greater. The connection with this consciousness helps us realize that our lives are intertwined with the lives of all beings, and it invites us to act with compassion and empathy. As the Buddhist philosopher Thich Nhat Hanh said: "When you look deeply, you see that you are not alone. You are the life of all beings."

Thus, by cultivating inner silence, we not only access Cosmic Consciousness but also become more aware of the interconnections that permeate existence. This recognition inspires us to live more consciously, to make decisions that respect and honor this interdependence. By connecting with universal energy, we realize that we are co-creators of reality, capable of influencing the world around us in meaningful ways.

Therefore, as you sit in silence, take a deep breath and allow yourself to dive into this transformative experience. Each moment of stillness is an opportunity to expand your awareness and connect with the essence of the cosmos. As the Greek philosopher Pythagoras said: "Silence is a friend who never betrays." May we, then, make this friend our ally, allowing inner silence to guide us toward deep understanding and the realization of the Cosmic Consciousness that dwells within each of us. Thus, by opening the portal of silence, we become not only listeners of our own soul but also messengers of the harmony and unity that permeate the universe.

THE PRACTICE OF GRATITUDE

A PATH TO COSMIC CONSCIOUSNESS

Gratitude is much more than a fleeting feeling; it is a transformative practice that deeply connects us with Cosmic Consciousness. In a world often dominated by worries and dissatisfactions, cultivating gratitude offers us a refreshing perspective, allowing us to appreciate the beauty and abundance that surround us. As the philosopher and essayist Ralph Waldo Emerson said: "Gratitude is the memory of the heart." By expressing gratitude, we not only remember the blessings in our lives but also open our hearts to a higher vibrational frequency, aligning ourselves with the energy of the universe.

Starting a gratitude journal is a powerful way to incorporate this practice into our daily lives. By dedicating a few minutes each day to jotting down three things we are grateful for, we begin to train our minds to focus on the positive. This practice, according to psychologist Amy C. Edmondson, can change the way we see the world: "Gratitude turns what we have into enough." Instead of focusing on lacks or difficulties, gratitude invites us to acknowledge and appreciate what we already have, creating a cycle of abundance and contentment.

Science also supports the benefits of gratitude. Studies show that people who practice gratitude regularly experience higher levels of happiness and well-being. Psychologist Robert Emmons, one of the leading researchers on gratitude, states: "Gratitude is a form of wisdom. We recognize that life is not an individual fight, but a gift that has been given to us by others." This perception not only connects us to others but also reminds us that we are part of something greater—a web of interconnections that unites us to Cosmic Consciousness.

The practice of gratitude helps us realign our vibrational frequency, allowing us to connect to a higher consciousness. When we express gratitude, we create a space of openness and receptivity, where the abundance of the universe can flow freely into our lives. The renowned writer and thinker Deepak Chopra reminds us that "gratitude is the key to abundance." By adopting this abundance mindset, we begin to attract more experiences and opportunities that resonate with this positive energy.

It is important to emphasize that gratitude is not only about grand moments or significant achievements. It is a practice that extends to the small details of everyday life—the aroma of morning coffee, a friend's smile, the beauty of a sunset. As the writer Melody Beattie said: "Gratitude is not just about responding to a blessing received, but an attitude that allows us to see the blessing in everything." This shift in perspective is what connects us directly to Cosmic Consciousness, allowing us to recognize the sacredness in every life experience.

When practicing gratitude, we also begin to cultivate empathy and compassion. We recognize that everyone faces challenges and that our journey is shared. The author and activist Brené Brown highlights that "gratitude is a practice that teaches us to live with courage, compassion, and connection." By allowing ourselves to feel and express gratitude, we not only change our own reality but also positively impact those around us, creating a domino effect of love and support.

As we delve deeper into this practice, it's essential to remember that gratitude is a state of being, not just a one-time activity. It can be said that it is a lifestyle that invites us to remain aware and mindful of the blessings that surround us. The philosopher and theologian Meister Eckhart emphasized: "If the only prayer you ever say in your entire life is 'thank you,' it will be enough." This simple yet powerful statement encapsulates the essence of gratitude. By adopting this attitude, we transform not only our lives but also the way we interact with the world.

Thus, as we begin the practice of gratitude, may we open

ourselves to the abundance of the universe and the Cosmic Consciousness within us. May each note in our gratitude journal become a celebration of life, a confirmation that we are part of something greater and more beautiful. Gratitude is not just a practice but a powerful portal that connects us to the love and light of the cosmos, allowing us to flourish in our true potential.

Ultimately, by nurturing gratitude in our hearts, we allow ourselves to flourish in our true potential. By nurturing our hearts, we become channels of light and love, radiating these qualities to the world around us. By practicing gratitude daily, we not only enrich our own lives but also contribute to the creation of a more harmonious and supportive environment. So, may we always remember the words of Oprah Winfrey: "Gratitude is one of the greatest healing powers there is." By embracing this practice, we are not only transforming our lives but also helping to transform the world, one act of gratitude at a time.

Ultimately, practices of energy alignment drive us to embrace our role as part of a greater whole. As the poet **Rumi said, "You are not the drop in the ocean, but the ocean in the drop."** By recognizing this truth, we are inspired to live more authentically, aligning our actions with universal energy and allowing Cosmic Consciousness to flow through us, in constant transformation and expansion.

NATURE AS REFUGE

A PATH TO COSMIC CONSCIOUSNESS

Nature, in its beauty and complexity, is one of the greatest mirrors of Cosmic Consciousness. By reconnecting with the natural environment, we are gently reminded of our interdependence with the whole; that we are integral parts of a vast and intricate system that sustains life. The philosopher and naturalist John Muir, known for his reverence for nature, stated: "When one is in harmony with nature, they will find their true essence." This quest for harmony is an invitation to explore the role that nature plays in our lives and how it can guide us toward a deeper understanding of ourselves and the universe.

In the hectic and stimulus-filled days of modern life, we often forget to pause and reconnect with the earth. Take time to walk in a park, feel the gentle breeze, listen to the birds' song, or simply gaze at the stars at night. These moments of contemplation are essential to remind us that we are part of something much greater.

As the poet William Wordsworth said: "Nature never hurries. Everything arrives in its own time, everything that waits." By adopting this slower and more mindful rhythm, we can open our hearts and minds to the wisdom nature offers us.

Nature is not just a backdrop; it is a source of vital energy that connects us to the cosmos. Feel the earth's energy beneath your feet, the texture of a tree's bark, the freshness of a drop of dew. Each of these elements carries intrinsic wisdom that invites us to reflect on our place in the universe. The writer and environmentalist Rachel Carson said: "Life is a dance between man and nature." This dance teaches us about the interconnectedness of all beings and the importance of respecting and caring for our planet.

When we allow ourselves to immerse in this sensory experience, we enter a state of expanded consciousness. Nature has the ability to elevate us beyond our daily concerns, allowing us to access a broader and deeper perspective on life. The scientist and philosopher Albert Einstein observed: "The mind that opens to a new idea never returns to its original size." By opening ourselves to the beauty and wisdom of nature, we expand our consciousness and become more receptive to the universal truths that surround us.

Moreover, the connection with nature can be profoundly healing. Studies show that spending time outdoors reduces stress, improves mental health, and increases the sense of well-being. The physician and author Dr. David Suzuki, an advocate for environmental preservation, stated: "Nature is our greatest teacher." By recognizing the importance of this connection, we can find refuge in forests, mountains, and rivers, where life pulses in its purest and most natural state.

On this path of reconnection, it is essential to remember that nature also teaches us about cycles and changes. The Greek philosopher Heraclitus said: "The only constant is change." Through the observation of seasons, plant growth, and animal migration, we are reminded that life is a continuous flow of transformations. This acceptance of impermanence helps us find peace in our own transitions and challenges.

Finally, by turning to nature as a refuge, we are making a conscious choice to honor our true essence and our place in the cosmos. In a world that often seems chaotic and disconnected, nature offers us a sacred space for reflection, healing, and reconnection. As the poet Rainer Maria Rilke said: "Nature is not a place to visit. It is home." May we, then, find our home in nature, allowing its wisdom to guide us on our journey of self-discovery and expansion of consciousness. In doing so, we not only reconnect with ourselves but also contribute to the preservation and harmony of the whole.

Energy Alignment Practices: Connecting Body and Spirit with Cosmic Consciousness

In a fast-paced world full of distractions, it is vital to find ways to reconnect with the essence of who we are. Energy alignment practices such as yoga, mindfulness, tai chi, qigong, swimming, long walks, and climbing offer not only a path to physical health but also an opportunity to integrate cosmic energy into our being. These ancestral and contemporary practices act as channels that allow us to access Cosmic Consciousness, making us feel part of a greater whole.

Yoga, for example, is one of those practices that stands out for its ability to unite body, mind, and spirit. Originating in India thousands of years ago, yoga is more than a series of physical postures; it is a philosophy that seeks inner harmony. As the sage Patanjali said, "Yoga is the cessation of the fluctuations of the mind." By practicing yoga, we learn to silence the mind and connect with our deepest essence, allowing the cosmic energy to flow through us. Asanas (postures) and pranayama (breathing techniques) not only promote physical health but also open the energy channels, facilitating the integration of Cosmic Consciousness into our being.

Another powerful practice is mindfulness, which invites us to be fully present in the moment. Jon Kabat-Zinn, one of the pioneers of mindfulness, defines the practice as "paying attention in a particular way, on purpose, in the present moment, and nonjudgmentally." By cultivating mindfulness, we learn to observe our thoughts and emotions without identifying with them, which allows us to access a deeper experience of life. This conscious presence helps us tune in to the energy of the universe, awakening a sense of interconnectedness with everything around us.

Chi and qigong are traditional Chinese practices that also aim to balance the vital energy (chi) in our bodies. Qigong, which means "energy work," combines gentle movement, breathing, and meditation, promoting health and well-being. The qigong master Mantak Chia taught that "energy flows where attention goes." Thus, by directing our attention to chi, we can not only strengthen our bodies but also connect to the universal energy around us. These practices make us channels for cosmic energy, allowing this life force to flow within us and help align body and spirit.

Activities like swimming, long walks, and climbing also play an important role in our energy alignment. Swimming, for example, allows us to move in a fluid environment, releasing tensions and connecting with water, a symbol of purification and renewal. The philosopher and writer Hermann Hesse said: "Water is the element of life." When we swim, we can feel this vital energy enveloping us, promoting a state of harmony and inner peace.

Long walks, especially in natural environments, offer a unique opportunity to reconnect with the Earth and cosmic energy. The naturalist John Muir stated: "In my experience, there is no better way to get to know nature than by walking." These walks not only strengthen our bodies but also allow us to breathe fresh air, absorb sunlight, and feel the energy of the ground under our feet. The connection with nature during these walks reminds us that we are part of a broader ecosystem and that this interdependence is fundamental to our well-being.

Climbing, on the other hand, challenges us to overcome our physical and mental limits. When climbing, we experience a deep connection with the rocks, air, and sky, evoking a feeling of freedom and accomplishment. The climber Reinhold Messner, famous for his high-altitude climbs, said: "The mountain is not an obstacle, but a means." Each challenge we face in climbing teaches us to trust ourselves and our ability to overcome adversity, a valuable lesson that extends to other areas of our lives.

As we commit to these practices of energy alignment, we begin to realize that we are more than just physical beings; we are manifestations of the cosmic energy flowing through us. This realization invites us to a state of expanded consciousness, where the separation between self and the universe dissolves. As the philosopher Alan Watts said: "No one can awaken a person who pretends to be asleep." By dedicating ourselves to practices that promote energy alignment, we awaken to the truth of our interconnectedness with all that exists.

These experiences transform us into channels of energy,

allowing Cosmic Consciousness to manifest in our lives. When we align our bodies and spirits, we not only enhance our physical and mental health but also become co-creators of the reality we live in. Through this connection, we can access an unlimited source of creativity, love, and wisdom, contributing to a more harmonious and conscious world.

Ultimately, practices of energy alignment drive us to embrace our role as part of a greater whole. As the poet Rumi said, "You are not the drop in the ocean, but the ocean in the drop." By recognizing this truth, we are inspired to live more authentically, aligning our actions with universal energy and allowing Cosmic Consciousness to flow through us, in constant transformation and expansion.

CONSCIOUS EATING

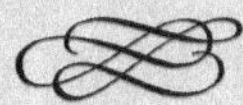

A PATH TO INTEGRAL HEALTH

Food is one of the fundamental bases of our existence. From the earliest childhood, we learn that we are what we eat. However, in a world dominated by convenience and haste, we often find ourselves consuming food unconsciously, choosing options that, despite being quick and accessible, can have devastating consequences for our physical, mental, and emotional health.

One of the most relevant aspects of healthy eating is the practice of intermittent and conscious eating. This approach not only values the quality of the food we ingest but also promotes a more positive and conscious relationship with food. The renowned poet and theologian Rumi said, "You are not a drop in the ocean. You are the ocean in a drop." This quote reminds us of the interconnectedness between us and the world around us, including what we choose to put into our bodies.

Conscious and healthy eating is a choice that results in significant physiological benefits. Studies show that a diet rich in fruits, vegetables, whole grains, and lean proteins can reduce the risk of chronic diseases such as diabetes, hypertension, and heart disease. On the other hand, a diet based on fast food, which is often high in refined sugars, trans fats, and sodium, is associated with a range of health issues, including obesity and metabolic disorders.

On a physiological level, intermittent fasting has also gained prominence for its potential benefits. The practice of restricting food intake to specific periods can promote weight loss, improve insulin sensitivity, and even increase longevity. As the physician and author Dr. Jason Fung states, "Fasting is not a diet, but an approach that allows the body to recover and regenerate."

Apart from the physical benefits, conscious and healthy eating also plays a crucial role in our emotional and psychological health. The link between what we eat and how we feel is undeniable. Nutrient-rich foods have the ability to positively influence our mood, while poor diets can contribute to anxiety and depression. The famous nutritionist and author Ellyn Satter said, "Food is a way of showing love, and we should treat it as such." This love is reflected in how we choose to nourish ourselves and the impact it has on our mental well-being.

On the other hand, unconscious eating, often associated with fast food consumption, can lead to a cycle of guilt and dissatisfaction. Eating quickly and without attention not only disconnects us from natural hunger and satiety cues but can also result in increased stress and anxiety. The psychologist and author Dr. Kelly McGonigal asserts that "stress is the body's response to disconnection." When we eat unconsciously, this disconnection is amplified, not just regarding food but with ourselves and our bodies.

The choice of a healthy and conscious diet also has significant social implications. By choosing fresh and sustainable foods, we support responsible farming practices and promote healthier communities. The famous activist and author Vandana Shiva says, "Food is the basis of culture, and culture defines us." By valuing the food we consume, we foster a sense of community and belonging, which is essential for social cohesion.

Furthermore, the practice of mindful eating can inspire changes within our social circles. By sharing healthy meals with friends and family, we promote an environment of support and encouragement, where everyone is encouraged to make healthier choices. As chef and activist Jamie Oliver said, "Food is a language that speaks to everyone. Through it, we can unite people."

In summary, healthy, intermittent, and conscious eating is a practice that goes beyond the simple act of eating. It invites us to reflect on our choices, to connect with our bodies, and to understand the impact our diet has on our health, emotions, and society as a whole. By adopting this approach, we not only nourish our bodies but also cultivate a lifestyle that promotes integral well-being, empathy, and social responsibility.

As the French philosopher and writer Jean-Paul Sartre said, "We are condemned to be free." This freedom allows us to choose not only what we put on our plates but also how we live our lives. By opting for healthy and conscious eating, we make a statement about who we are and what we value. Each meal becomes an opportunity to nourish our body and mind, to honor our health, and to contribute to a more sustainable and supportive world.

Therefore, as we reflect on our dietary choices, may we embrace this freedom with responsibility, cultivating a harmonious relationship with food, our body, and society. Eating becomes a self-care ritual, where each bite is a step towards a fuller and more meaningful life. By nourishing the body consciously, we also feed our soul, creating a virtuous cycle that benefits not only ourselves but everyone around us. May we, thus, be agents of change in our lives and the lives of others, promoting a culture of health, well-being, and connection.

The journey of mindful eating is not just about what we choose to eat but about how these choices shape our existence and impact the world we inhabit. It is, therefore, an invitation to transformation, where each of us has the power to make a difference, starting with the plate.

THE ART OF INTENTION

SHAPING REALITY WITH COSMIC CONSCIOUSNESS

Intention is one of the most powerful forces we possess. Since time immemorial, philosophers, spiritualists, and scientists have recognized the transformative potential of intention in our lives. As the renowned author and spirituality teacher Deepak Chopra said, "Intention is a field of energy that influences matter." This statement invites us to reflect on the depth of this power. When we set clear and specific intentions, we begin to shape our reality and align with the Cosmic Consciousness, opening the doors to a world of infinite possibilities.

The practice of writing our intentions is a fundamental step in this process. When we put our wishes and goals on paper, we are giving form and substance to them. This action is not merely symbolic; it is a way of anchoring our aspirations in physical reality. The writer and thinker Paulo Coelho, in his famous book *The Alchemist*, reminds us that "when you desire something, all the universe conspires to help you achieve it." This quote resonates deeply with the concept that, by expressing our intentions, we create a vibration that echoes throughout the universe, attracting the necessary circumstances and opportunities for their realization.

Visualization is another powerful tool in the art of intention. By visualizing our intentions as if they have already been realized, we are not only activating the power of manifestation but also connecting to the universe's vibration. The renowned psychologist and author Shakti Gawain, in her book *Creative Visualization*, emphasizes that "visualization is a way of creating a clear mental image of what you want." When we allow ourselves to feel the emotions associated with achieving our desires, we are indeed vibrating at the frequency necessary for these intentions to materialize. Quantum science also supports this idea; quantum physics suggests that our observations of the world influence its reality. Therefore, by focusing our attention and energy on intentions, we become co-creators of our lives.

It is important to remember that intention is not just a manifestation tool; it also becomes a moral and ethical guide in our lives. When we set intentions that align with our deepest values, we become more aware of the impact of our actions on the world around us. Activist and writer Marianne Williamson said, "Our deepest fear is not that we are inadequate. Our deepest fear is that we are powerful beyond measure." This quote reminds us that by aligning with authentic and true intentions, we not only shape our lives but also contribute to a more enlightened and conscious world.

The regular practice of setting intentions, combined with visualization, can become a powerful ritual. By dedicating a daily moment to reflect on our intentions, we cultivate a space of clarity and purpose in our lives. This allows us to adjust our paths and choices, ensuring that we remain aligned with what we truly desire. The philosopher Henry David Thoreau said, "The only way to live is by finding what is true for you and living it." Thus, by committing to our intentions, we are living according to our deepest truth.

Furthermore, the practice of intention can be expanded through meditation and mindfulness. By quieting the mind and tuning into the present, we create a deeper connection with our essence and with the Cosmic Consciousness. Meditation allows us to hear the inner voice that guides us, helping us refine our intentions according to what truly resonates within our being. The writer and mystic Rumi reminds us that "your task is not to seek for love, but merely to seek and find all the barriers within yourself that you have built against it." This internal quest is what allows us to align our intentions with our true essence. Through meditation and reflection, we can dismantle the barriers that separate us from our most authentic desires. In doing so, we find not only clarity but also a profound sense of purpose. When we truly connect with our essence, our intentions become a genuine reflection of who we are and what we wish to contribute to the world.

Thus, by cultivating the art of intention, we not only shape our individual realities but also create a network of energy and consciousness that extends beyond us. Each positive intention we emit resonates in the universe, contributing to a more loving and harmonious environment. As the great thinker Mahatma Gandhi said, "The change we wish to see in the world begins with us." Therefore, by striving to live our intentions with authenticity and passion, we become beacons of light, inspiring others to do the same.

In summary, the art of intention is a powerful practice that invites us to be co-creators of our lives, aligning ourselves with Cosmic Consciousness and manifesting our deepest desires. By writing, visualizing, and meditating on our intentions, we cultivate a space of personal and collective transformation, where each of us has the potential to contribute to a more conscious and vibrant world. And thus, the journey of intention becomes not just a personal quest but a shared mission of love and evolution.

FIND YOUR PURPOSE

THE MEANING OF OUR JOURNEY

Life is a brief but extraordinary journey. Amid the complexities and challenges we face, one of the most fundamental aspects we can discover is our purpose. "Life is really simple, but we insist on making it complicated," Confucius said. And that simplicity can be found in the clarity of purpose. When we have a defined meaning for our existence, we can navigate through the turbulences of life with more ease and confidence.

Finding a purpose is like receiving a map that guides us toward our goals. It gives us direction, allowing our decisions to align with our values and aspirations. Without it, we may get lost in distractions that take us away from our true essence. As Viktor Frankl, psychiatrist and Holocaust survivor, said, "Life never becomes unbearable by circumstance, but only by lack of meaning and purpose." These words echo the importance of knowing where we want to go.

Life, with its inevitable difficulties, requires resilience. Having a clear purpose motivates us to face challenges with courage. When we know why we do what we do, we find an inner strength that drives us to move forward. Frankl also stated, "When we can no longer change a situation, we are challenged to change ourselves." This capacity for adaptation is often fueled by an understanding of our purpose.

Finding a purpose is not a solitary journey. It connects us to other people who share similar interests and values. The sense of community that arises from this connection is fundamental to our emotional well-being. As Helen Keller said, "Alone we can do so little; together we can do so much." Our purposes unite us around meaningful causes, creating significant and lasting bonds.

When we engage in activities that we find meaningful, we experience a deep sense of satisfaction. The pleasure that comes from living according to our purpose not only enhances our quality of life but also helps us feel that we are making a difference in the world. The writer Maya Angelou said, "You cannot control all the events that happen around you, but you can control your attitude towards them." This positive attitude is often fueled by the recognition that we are living meaningfully.

The search for a purpose is also a journey of self-discovery. Reflecting on what we truly value, what we are passionate about, and what motivates us helps us better understand ourselves. "Know thyself," one of the oldest teachings of philosophy, remains an essential guide in our quest for meaning. Self-knowledge is a powerful tool that allows us to live authentically.

We live on an extraordinarily abundant planet. The natural beauty, diverse cultures, and unique experiences that surround us are a testament to the richness of life. Finding a purpose allows us to value this diversity, encouraging us to explore, learn, and grow. As Albert Einstein said, "Life is like riding a bicycle. To keep your balance, you must keep moving." This movement is essential for appreciating and taking advantage of all that the world has to offer.

A purpose often inspires us to contribute to the well-being of society and the environment. Our actions can have a positive impact, making the world a better place for future generations. "The best way to find yourself is to lose yourself in the service of others," said Mahatma Gandhi. This altruism, when guided by a purpose, creates a virtuous cycle of growth and transformation.

Being aware of our purpose helps us live fully in the present. Instead of worrying excessively about the future or lamenting the past, we can focus on meaningful actions that bring joy and satisfaction now. "The past is no longer under our control, and the future is in our hands," said the philosopher Søren Kierkegaard. This perspective allows us to appreciate each moment as an opportunity for growth and learning.

The search for a purpose involves learning and personal growth. As we dedicate ourselves to better understanding our passions and skills, we become more adaptable and resilient. Every step we take toward our purpose is an opportunity to expand our horizons, acquire new skills, and challenge our limiting beliefs. As Ralph Waldo Emerson said, "The only person you are destined to become is the person you decide to be." Therefore, by embracing this journey of self-discovery and development, we not only find our purpose but also transform ourselves into the best version of us.

THE CALL TO COURAGE AND ACTION

The Journey Towards Cosmic Consciousness

Cosmic Consciousness is always present, waiting for us to take the initiative to connect with it. This call urges us to awaken to the grandeur of our being and explore the depths of our existence. The philosopher Alan Watts reminds us that the true journey of discovery is not about seeking new landscapes, but having new eyes. This shift in perspective is essential for us to perceive the infinite possibilities around us, allowing us to establish a deeper connection with the universe.

To align ourselves energetically and set clear intentions, it is necessary to shape our reality. By harmonizing our energies with our surroundings, we can discern what truly resonates with our essence. Gary Zukav states that intention is the universe's creative power, and by setting them clearly, we begin to open doors for the manifestation of our desires. This practice transcends the individual, becoming part of the fabric of collective consciousness.

It is important to recognize that the first step towards the unknown can be terrifying, but it is in this space of discomfort that true growth occurs. The courage to venture beyond the limits of the familiar leads us to extraordinary discoveries. Paulo Coelho expresses this idea by saying that the only way to achieve the impossible is to believe it is possible. By allowing the universe to guide us, we open the doors to a flow of experiences that enlightens and transforms us.

Courage is an essential component of the human experience. It is the force that motivates us to step out of our comfort zone, face challenges, and seek authenticity in our lives. Without courage, many of history's significant achievements, from personal advancements to social transformations, would never have occurred. Aristotle highlighted that courage is the first of human qualities because it guarantees all the others.

Courage is not the absence of fear, but the ability to act despite it. It is this action that leads us to discover our true potential. Nelson Mandela, an icon of the fight for equality, said that courage is not the absence of fear but the triumph over it. This perspective reminds us that we all face insecurities, but it is in overcoming these obstacles that we find true strength.

A remarkable example is the life of Malala Yousafzai, a young Pakistani who became a global symbol of the fight for girls' right to education. After surviving a brutal attack, Malala had the courage to rise and continue her fight, inspiring millions with her famous phrase: "One book, one pen, one child, and one teacher can change the world." Her courage to act had a lasting impact.

When courage is allied with action, it becomes a transformative force. Martin Luther King Jr. reminds us of the urgency to question: "What are you doing for others?" This reflection on each person's role in society highlights that the courage to act for the collective well-being not only transforms others' lives but also enriches our own lives.

Rosa Parks, by refusing to give up her seat on a bus, sparked a movement that would change the face of civil rights in the United States. Her determination and courage were fundamental in the fight for equality. As she said, "I am not tired. I am tired of being treated as if I were nothing."

The courage to act is a path to self-discovery and personal growth. By making bold decisions, we begin to realize the strength that resides within us. Maya Angelou reminds us that, although we cannot control all events, we can control our attitude towards them. This choice of how to react is a powerful act of courage.

Contemporary examples of people who have overcome significant adversities, such as serious illnesses or financial crises, also illustrate how the courage to act can transform lives. These stories of resilience show that each step, even if small, is an affirmation of courage, creating a domino effect that inspires others to fight for their own lives and dreams.

Courage and action are essential for us to achieve our maximum potential. Each of us has the ability to face fears and act in pursuit of goals. By doing so, we not only change our own lives but also influence the world around us. Ralph Waldo Emerson reminds us that the only person we are destined to become is the person we decide to be. Therefore, the courage to act is the first step in shaping our reality and contributing to a more conscious and harmonious world. By allowing ourselves to dream big and act decisively, we attract into our lives experiences and opportunities that may once have seemed unattainable. It is in this space of courage and action that Cosmic Consciousness becomes more accessible, revealing itself in every choice we make.

Throughout our journey, we will be challenged to confront our fears and limitations. However, it is in this internal struggle that we find the strength to redefine and grow. As the philosopher Friedrich Nietzsche said, "He who has a why to live can bear almost any how." By finding purpose in our actions, we not only transform ourselves but also inspire those around us to do the same.

Ultimately, the true essence of courage lies in the ability to act with purpose and integrity. Each step we take towards our personal truth is a step towards the expansion of Cosmic

Consciousness. By uniting with this universal energy, we promote not only our own growth but also that of all humanity.

May we, therefore, respond to this call to action with determination and boldness, guided by the light of consciousness and the strength of courage. Together, we can create a world where authenticity and compassion reign, and where each of us is free to be exactly who we were born to be.

THE CREATIVE COSMIC CONSCIOUSNESS

"We are all travelers on a cosmic journey – Stardust, swirling and dancing in the whirlpools and eddies of the infinite." — **Deepak Chopra**

In the depths of the universe, beyond the stars and galaxies that twinkle like diamonds in a vast black mantle, resides the Creative Cosmic Consciousness. This entity—or perhaps better, this essence—is the primordial source of all that exists: the spark that ignites life, the inspiration that shapes matter, and the energy that permeates the soul of every being. It is a concept that transcends the limitations of language and reason, a mystery that unfolds in layers of beauty and complexity, like the petals of a rose that slowly open to the morning sun.

On this planet that I call the "Planet of Magic and Miracles," the Cosmic Consciousness manifests in surprising and enchanting ways. Here, abundance is not just a material reality but a state of mind. The earth, rich and generous, offers fruits and flowers that dance to the rhythm of the breeze, as if each plant were in communion with the music of the cosmos. The rivers, in their endless dance, reflect the sky and stars, as if the universe itself were gazing into the mirror of existence.

But how is it possible for such a vast and intangible consciousness to have shaped our world in such an extraordinary manner? The answer lies in the interconnectedness between all beings and the ability of each one of them to access this source of creativity. When an artist paints, he does not merely apply paint to the canvas; he tunes into the frequency of the Cosmic Consciousness, allowing the beauty of the universe to manifest through his hands. When a scientist makes a discovery, he is not just analyzing data; he is unraveling the secrets that the very consciousness of the cosmos has left as clues, as if each formula were a verse in a cosmic poem.

However, living in such a magical world also implies challenges. Abundance and beauty can sometimes be overshadowed by doubt, fear, and mental scarcity. Cosmic Consciousness, while also being a creator, is a mirror that reflects our emotions and thoughts. If we allow negativity and a lack of faith to settle in our hearts, we can obscure the light that surrounds us. Thus, the true miracle is not just external creation but the internal transformation that each of us must undertake to align with the flow of cosmic abundance.

Imagine a moment when, upon waking in the morning, we connect with this Consciousness. We breathe deeply, allowing vital energy to flow through us, recognizing that we are part of a greater whole. In this state of expanded consciousness, each action can become a sacred ritual. Each relationship, a cosmic dance. Each challenge, an opportunity to grow and learn. Magic is not just something observed but something lived and expressed in every thought, word, and action.

For this connection to become a tangible reality, we need to cultivate practices that help us tune into that frequency. Meditation, contemplation of nature, art, and music are portals that lead us to this dimension. When we allow ourselves to be creators in our own lives, we access the abundance that Cosmic Consciousness offers us. Each of us is a potential genius, capable of manifesting miracles in our daily lives.

Finally, the Creative Cosmic Consciousness is not a distant idea but a living presence that inhabits each of us. By recognizing our own divinity and our role as co-creators, we can transform our planet into a true home of magic and miracles. This is the call: to awaken to the beauty that surrounds us, to cultivate gratitude and creativity, and to let Cosmic

Consciousness guide us on our journey. Thus, together, we can reveal the unlimited potential that resides in our planet and in our hearts.

THE DANCE OF THE COSMOS: CAUSE AND EFFECT

The universe, in its infinite vastness, operates under the main law that governs all its interactions: the law of cause and effect. Each action triggers a reaction; each thought generates a vibration; each emotion emanates an energy that propagates through the fabric of the cosmos. In this immense cosmic stage, human life, with its brevity and ephemerality, may seem insignificant. However, it is precisely this transience that makes our moments so valuable and worthy of reflection.

Imagine the immensity of time that preceded the existence of humanity. Stars were born and died, galaxies collided and separated, and in this vast cosmic ballet, our passage on Earth is like a whisper in the wind. Yet, it is in this brief breath that lies the opportunity to make a difference. Every day, we have the choice of how to spend our time—the most precious resource we possess. And this choice must be guided by passion, by what we truly love.

When we dedicate ourselves to what we love, our essence is reflected in our actions. The energy we put into our creations, whether a product, a service, or an interaction, resonates in the universe. This energy, pure and vibrant, is not lost; instead, it transforms, expands, and connects with other like energies. When we infuse love and intention into our work, this energy is transmitted directly into the space that surrounds us. And so, what we create becomes more than a simple transaction; it becomes an extension of ourselves.

The love we put into our activities not only elevates the quality of what we do but also attracts those who seek that same vibration. Products and services imbued with positive energy resonate with others, becoming beacons that light the way for those in search of something more. Success is not just a matter of profit; it is a natural consequence of aligning with what we love and sharing that passion with the world. When people feel the authenticity and intention behind what we offer, they connect. This creates a network of well-being that extends beyond the boundaries of commerce and touches the lives of all involved.

Meanwhile, we live in a world that often educates us to operate like robots, to follow established patterns, and to sacrifice our time and energy in exchange for a salary that barely covers our basic needs. This reality, which affects our psychological, emotional, and social well-being, is a reflection of a system that prioritizes productivity over passion. Most of us have been conditioned to believe that work should be an obligation, a burdensome task to be endured, and not an expression of our true essence.

But the truth is that today, we hold the power of information in our hands. We live in an era of accessible knowledge, where the awakening of consciousness is a real possibility. We can, and should, question this narrative. What prevents us from living a life of authenticity and purpose? What prevents us from breaking free from the shackles of a job that does not nurture us? It's time to rewrite this story.

The abundance of this planet is not just a material reality; it is a spiritual truth. For us to achieve the balance and equality we all desire, it is essential that each of us recognizes our worth and the importance of living in harmony with what we truly love. When we begin to see work as an extension of ourselves, as an opportunity to share our passions, we can create a virtuous cycle of cause and effect, where everyone benefits.

Imagine a world where people wake up every morning excited to do what they love, where creativity and collaboration flow freely. Visualize communities where success is measured not only in financial terms but also in terms of happiness, health, and fulfillment. This world is possible, but it requires each of us to take responsibility for our choices and the energy we emit.

By embracing the law of cause and effect in our lives, we can transform not only our own destiny but also that of everyone around us. Change begins with us, and every small step towards what we love reverberates through the cosmos, creating waves that can inspire others to do the same. Thus, by deciding to live with intention and love, we will be contributing to a more balanced and abundant future—a true paradise where everyone can thrive. This choice, although it may seem small in the grand scheme of the cosmos, is, in reality, a seed that can germinate into significant transformations. Every act of kindness, every moment of dedication to what we love, creates an echo that resonates through time and space, influencing not only our lives but also the lives of those around us.

As we delve deeper into this journey of self-discovery and authenticity, we begin to realize that we are part of an interconnected web of human experiences. Every interaction we have, every smile we share, and every act of love we offer contributes to the collective energy of our world. This energy is not static; it flows, transforms, and multiplies, creating a domino effect that can alter realities and inspire changes on scales we often cannot imagine.

And, as more individuals awaken to this truth, the possibility of a new collective consciousness emerges. Imagine entire communities coming together not just to work, but to celebrate life, to explore their passions, and to support each other on their journeys. Instead of competitors, we become collaborators, joining forces to create something greater than ourselves. The energy we put into our efforts, fueled by love and passion, becomes a powerful fuel for innovation, creativity, and prosperity.

However, for this transformation to occur, it is essential that we recognize and face the challenges that arise on our path. We need to deconstruct the limiting beliefs imposed on us, question the paradigms that keep us trapped in a cycle of dissatisfaction, and, above all, cultivate the courage to follow our hearts. This may require a conscious effort, but the reward is immeasurable. When we allow ourselves to dream and act according to those dreams, we begin to redefine what it means to live fully.

The path to this new reality is not free of obstacles. The fear of the unknown, ingrained behavior patterns, and social pressures can create resistance to change. However, just like stars that shine amid darkness, the light of our passion can guide us through uncertainties. By surrounding ourselves with people who share our vision, supporting each other, and celebrating every victory, no matter how small, we strengthen this light and make it more radiant.

It is time to free ourselves from the chains that bind us to a monotonous and unsatisfying existence. It is time to recognize that we are creators of our own reality, co-authors of our stories. By embracing the law of cause and effect and understanding that every choice counts, we can build a legacy that endures beyond our lives—a legacy of love, of passion, and an unwavering commitment to what truly matters.

Thus, I invite you, dear reader, to reflect on your own life. What do you love? What makes your heart beat fast? How can you infuse your energy and intention into the activities you carry out? The universe is listening, and your actions, no matter how small, have the power to create waves of change. Therefore, dare to dream, dare to act, and above all, dare to love. Because, in the grand scheme of the cosmos, love is the most powerful force of all—and the true essence of what it means to be human.

Together, we can transform our reality, one act of love at a time, until the echo of our actions reverberates throughout the cosmos, creating a world where every being can flourish, where abundance is the norm, and where life is celebrated in all its forms. This is the call of our time; this is the promise of our future.

THE GENIUS OF AUTHENTIC LIFE

In the vast universe of human experience, where each of us is a traveler in search of meaning, emerges the figure of the "Genius of Authentic Life." This genius is not a magical entity that grants wishes but rather a palpable presence that resides within us, waiting to be awakened. It is the personification of authentic love, inner peace, contagious joy, sincere compassion, unshakable resilience, vibrant freedom, and prosperity that transcends materialism.

Throughout life, we are often confronted with the duality between what is imposed on us by the external world and what we truly desire within. The genius invites us to break these barriers and discover life experiences that truly resonate with our essence. The first lesson we learn when embracing the genius is that authentic love is not just an emotion; it is a state of being. This love manifests in relationships that do not depend on conditions, where the simple act of being present is enough to nurture and strengthen bonds. By surrendering to this love, we learn to value the other, to see beauty in imperfections, and to celebrate the uniqueness of each individual.

As we delve deeper into this journey, we find peace that comes from within. It is not a peace conquered through the absence of conflicts but rather a serenity that allows us to face storms with a calm heart. This peace becomes a beacon in times of uncertainty, guiding us not only in our interactions with others but also in our relationship with ourselves. The practice of meditation, for example, can be seen as a tool that helps us connect with this genius, providing us with moments of reflection and self-awareness.

Joy, then, blossoms as a result of this connection. Not the fleeting joy found in superficial pleasures, but a deep joy that arises from gratitude for the small things in life. The genius teaches us that true joy is a choice; it is the decision to see the world through a positive lens, to find beauty even in the most challenging situations. A walk in nature, a smile exchanged with a stranger, or a moment of silence in appreciation can become inexhaustible sources of joy.

Compassion, in turn, is the thread that weaves our experiences of love and joy. The genius inspires us to look at the suffering of others with empathy, to reach out a hand to others without expecting anything in return. The practice of compassion not only transforms lives but also transforms us. In such a polarized world, where divisions seem to be the norm, compassion invites us to see beyond differences and connect on a deeper level.

However, life is not free of challenges. Here is where resilience becomes a fundamental ally. The genius teaches us that resilience is not just the ability to recover but the ability to grow and learn from adversity. Each obstacle becomes an opportunity to strengthen our character and expand our worldview. Resilience is cultivated through practices that allow us to face our fears and uncertainties, turning each fall into a push to rise stronger.

Freedom, often understood as the absence of limitations, is an internal experience. The genius guides us to realize that true freedom is not in escaping external shackles but in freeing our minds from limiting beliefs and judgments. This freedom allows us to live authentically, expressing our desires and yearnings without fear of what others will think. When we free ourselves from external expectations, we begin to dance to the rhythm of our own life.

Finally, prosperity is revealed as a state of abundance that goes beyond the material. The genius teaches us that prosperity is a reflection of the quality of our experiences and the depth of our relationships. It's about creating a legacy of love, compassion, and resilience that can be passed on to future generations. When we live authentically, we attract opportunities that nourish not only our material needs but also our deepest aspirations.

Thus, by embracing the genius of authentic life, we are invited to live experiences that resonate with love, peace, joy, compassion, resilience, freedom, and prosperity. Each of us carries within us this spark of authenticity, ready to be ignited. By allowing the inner genius to manifest, we begin to realize that our lives are not just a series of random events but an intricate tapestry woven with the threads of experiences lived with intention and love.

Thus, as travelers on a shared journey, we are called to explore not only what is external but also what resides within our being. This exploration leads us to a deeper understanding of ourselves and others around us. The journey of the genius of authentic life is about becoming aware of our emotions, thoughts, and actions, allowing us to live with a clarity that illuminates the path not only for ourselves but for those who cross our path.

As we delve into this state of awareness, we begin to notice that each interaction becomes an opportunity for learning and growth. A simple act of kindness can create waves of compassion that reverberate through time and space. Resilience becomes a driving force that propels us forward, even when the winds of life blow adversely. It is in this dance between acceptance and transformation that we find true freedom—the ability to be who we are, without the weight of external expectations or internal insecurities.

In this interconnected world, prosperity expands when we choose to share our experiences and learnings. When a heart loves authentically, it inspires others to do the same. The genius reminds us that by nurturing an environment of support and empathy, we not only enrich our own lives but also sow the seeds for a more harmonious future. Prosperity becomes a continuous cycle, where each act of generosity brings with it fruits of abundance and growth.

However, it is important to remember that this journey is not linear. There will be moments of doubt, insecurity, and even despair. The genius teaches us that these moments are not failures but essential parts of our development. They offer us the opportunity to reflect, reassess, and be reborn with a new perspective. The true beauty of life lies in its imperfection, and it is in this imperfection that we find genuine connection with others and with ourselves.

Therefore, by embracing the genius of authentic life, we are called to create a legacy of love, peace, and compassion. Our experiences intertwine, forming a vibrant network of support and understanding. Together, we can transform not only our lives but also the society around us. With every step we take, with every choice we make, we are reminded that true magic lies not in granted wishes but in fully living the life we are given, with authenticity and purpose.

May we commit to living with the awareness that we are co-creators of our reality. May we not only seek our own life experiences in authentic love, peace, joy, compassion, resilience, freedom, and prosperity but also inspire others to do the same. After all, life is a beautiful journey, and each of us has the power to be the genius who transforms not only their own story but also the world around them.

As we commit to living authentically, we are called to cultivate a space for dialogue and understanding. We need to remember that in such a diverse and multifaceted world, every voice has its value, and every story deserves to be heard. It is in this rich exchange of experiences that we find opportunities for mutual growth and collective learning.

With this, each of us can become an agent of change, not only in our communities but also in broader spheres. By coming together around causes that resonate in our hearts, we can create movements that generate significant impact. Solidarity and empathy become the keys that open doors to a more just and equal future.

Moreover, by embracing our vulnerability and sharing our struggles, we create space for others to do the same. This courage to be authentic generates a cycle of support that can transform lives. Instead of hiding behind masks, we can celebrate the beauty of imperfections that make us human. It is in this space of security that true connection is formed, and together we can overcome challenges that once seemed insurmountable.

And so, as we look to the future, we are reminded that every day is a new opportunity to make a difference. May we wake up with the intention of being the light that illuminates the path for others, of cultivating an environment where love and acceptance thrive. May our actions, no matter how small, be seeds of hope and inspiration, germinating in hearts willing to dream and act.

The journey of the genius of authentic life is not just an individual pursuit; it is an invitation to collectivity. May we walk together, side by side, always ready to support each other, always ready to celebrate achievements, big and small. Because, in the end, it is this union that transforms the world —a gesture, a word, an act of love from each of us. And thus, the magic of being human reveals itself in its purest form: in the ability to love, to dream, and to create a legacy that resonates for generations.

THE AWAKENING OF CONSCIOUSNESS: KNOWING YOURSELF

Life, this extraordinary gift offered to us, is like a vast ocean of possibilities. In each wave that forms, a new opportunity for learning and growth awaits us. Rumi, the famous Persian poet, said: "Your task is not to seek for love, but simply to seek and find all the barriers within yourself that you have built." This call to introspection is one of the keys to the awakening of consciousness.

From a young age, we are bombarded with expectations, beliefs, and norms that shape our worldview. However, how can we really know ourselves if we are constantly navigating the murky waters of others' opinions? It is essential that, at some point in our lives, we pause, look within, and allow ourselves to discover our true essence. As Carl Jung wisely observed: "Who looks outside, dreams; who looks inside, awakes."

This process of self-discovery is often a solitary journey and, at the same time, deeply connective. By allowing ourselves to explore our thoughts, feelings, and experiences, we begin to realize that we are more than just the labels others impose on us. We are, indeed, a collection of stories, hopes, fears, and dreams. The writer Maya Angelou stated: "I've learned that people will forget what you said, forget what you did, but never forget how you made them feel." This truth resonates deeply when we consider that, by knowing ourselves, we also understand how we can impact the lives of those around us.

Self-awareness is not just an act of introspection but also of acceptance. Accepting our faults and limitations is as vital as celebrating our victories and achievements. This balance is what makes us human, and it is, in fact, one of the greatest forms of self-love. As the philosopher Epictetus said: "It's not things that disturb us, but our opinion about them." Therefore, the first step to freedom is to free ourselves from the opinions that imprison us.

As we delve deeper into this journey of self-knowledge, it is essential to be open to continuous learning. Life is a school, and each experience, whether positive or negative, brings valuable lessons. The renowned author Paulo Coelho reminds us: "When you want something, all the universe conspires to help you achieve it." This conspiracy is not only external; it is also internal. When we commit to understanding who we are, the universe aligns, and opportunities manifest in ways we never could have imagined.

Understanding oneself is also a call to action. As we decipher what we truly want and need, we are driven to act towards these truths. This action can manifest in different forms: career changes, healthier relationships, or even the pursuit of new hobbies that nourish our soul. As the philosopher Simone de Beauvoir said: "By changing life, we change the world." It is in this spirit that, by knowing ourselves, we not only transform our lives but also contribute to the collective evolution of humanity.

Finally, the awakening of consciousness is an invitation to gratitude. By recognizing the beauty in life's nuances, we learn to value every moment, every challenge, and every joy. Gratitude connects us with the present, allowing us to live fully. "Gratitude is not only the greatest of virtues but the mother of all others," said Cicero, reminding us that this feeling is the foundation of a meaningful life.

Thus, as we embark on this journey of self-knowledge, let us remember that every step taken is a step towards a more authentic and fulfilling life. Self-awareness is not a destination but a continuous journey, a dance between who we are and who we aspire to be. And, as the philosopher Seneca said, "Life is long if you know how to use it." Therefore, let us use this life to explore the vast universe that resides within us and to celebrate our uniqueness in this great puzzle called humanity.

DISCOVERING WHO WE ARE

The journey of self-discovery is one of the most fascinating and, at the same time, challenging experiences I have ever undertaken. For me, it all began with simple but profoundly unsettling questions: "Who am I? What makes me happy? What are my talents and passions?" I remember a moment when I asked myself these questions while looking out the window, observing the world outside. The answers seemed distant, as if they were hidden under layers of expectations and obligations.

These questions, which at first glance may seem trivial, became the pillars that sustain my being. The philosopher Socrates said, "Know yourself," a piece of advice that echoed in my mind for years. This call to introspection resonated within me and urged me to seek not only in the external world but also within myself. The truth is that, from a very young age, I was encouraged to learn about the world around me—mathematics, sciences, languages—but I was rarely offered the opportunity to explore my inner world.

Why does this happen? Why aren't there dedicated spaces for self-knowledge in schools and homes? Throughout my life, I've realized that most people are not comfortable discussing their emotions or exploring their identities. And this made me reflect on the importance of introducing self-knowledge practices from childhood. Activities like meditation, art, and reflective writing can be powerful tools to help not only the young but all of us connect with our emotions and better understand who we truly are.

Experiencing meditation was one of the first steps I took on this journey. At first, it was difficult to silence the mind and allow myself to feel. However, as I persisted, I discovered an internal space of peace and clarity. As the author and teacher Thich Nhat Hanh said, "Peace is every step we take. If we are aware, peace will become a part of us." This practice began to reveal layers of my identity that had been hidden until then. I began to understand that I am not just what I do, but also what I feel and how I connect with others.

Moreover, reflective writing became a powerful ally in my quest for self-knowledge. By putting my thoughts and emotions on paper, I was able to see what had once been just a confused whirlwind in my mind. "Writing is the painting of the voice," said Voltaire, and this statement never seemed so true to me. Through writing, I began to express not only my experiences but also my hopes and fears. Each word revealed a little more about who I am, and this revelation was both liberating and transformative.

The art of cooking and pastry has become an essential vehicle in my journey of self-discovery. From a very young age, I learned the magic of flavors, textures, and colors, and the importance of putting love into everything I touch. Each recipe became an opportunity to create something special, where the combination of ingredients not only satisfied the palate but also nourished the soul. Because when we love what we are doing, it is only possible to be truly in the present moment. As they say, it's possible to "be in the zone," where creativity flows and the connection with what we do becomes intense. This dedication to cooking allowed me to explore emotions and experiences, and by sharing my dishes with others, I discovered a new dimension of human connection that enriched not only my life but also those who sat at the table with me.

Throughout this journey, I realized that self-discovery is not a destination but a continuous process. Sometimes the answers I seek reveal themselves quickly; other times, they hide, challenging me to continue the search. There is no manual to follow, but each step taken brings me closer to the truth about who I am.

In the end, I realize that true happiness does not reside solely in external achievements, but in the ability to live in authenticity. Writer and philosopher Ralph Waldo Emerson said, "The only way to have a friend is to be one." This applies to ourselves as well: the only way to truly know ourselves is to accept and love ourselves as we are. This acceptance brings with it a freedom I never imagined possible.

Therefore, as I continue this journey of discovery, I invite you to join me. Let us question, explore, and celebrate who we are. After all, life is an incredible opportunity to know ourselves and become the best version of ourselves. And so, together, we can illuminate the path for those who are still seeking their own truths.

THE PURPOSE AND THE CONNECTION WITH THE WHOLE

The search for purpose is a journey that has guided humanity since time immemorial. Plato, in his reflections, stated that "the greatest mistake a man can make is to sacrifice his health for anything else." This statement is not limited to physical health but also to spiritual and emotional health, which are nourished by understanding our place in the world and the impact we have around us. Understanding why we are here and what our role is in this vast universe is a question that, though complex, can be approached through the small actions we take daily.

The connection with the whole is a concept that resonates deeply within each of us. When we encourage children to engage in volunteer activities or explore their communities, we open a door for them to see themselves as part of something greater. It is an opportunity to cultivate empathy and social responsibility. As Mahatma Gandhi said: "The true measure of any society can be found in how it treats its most disadvantaged members." This principle applies not only to adults but also to children, who have the potential to become agents of change from an early age.

Imagine a child who, by participating in a community gardening project, not only learns about the life cycle of plants but also about the importance of collaboration and caring for the environment. Each seed planted becomes a symbol of hope and renewal, a metaphor for personal and social growth. By feeling part of this process, children begin to realize that their actions, no matter how small, have a significant impact. "Small acts, when multiplied by millions of people, can transform the world," said Howard Zinn, and it is with this mindset that we must cultivate awareness in new generations.

The connection with the whole also helps us understand that purpose is not a destination but a journey. It is a continuous process of discovery and rediscovery. As we engage in different activities, meet people, learn new skills, and broaden our perspectives, we grow. As the philosopher and writer Ralph Waldo Emerson said: "The only way to have a friend is to be one." This quote invites us to reflect on how, by giving of ourselves, we receive so much in return, creating bonds that connect us to each other and to the world.

Moreover, as we contemplate the idea that each of us has a unique mission, we must remember that this mission often intertwines with the needs of the world. In a time when society faces global challenges, it is imperative that new generations are educated not only to be successful but also to be conscious and supportive. The writer and activist Maya Angelou said: "I have learned that people will forget what you said, people will forget what you did, but they will never forget how you made them feel." This power to transform lives, even on a small scale, is a legacy we must pass on.

Volunteering activities can serve as a starting point for this journey of self-discovery. By helping others, children not only learn about compassion and altruism but also develop skills that will be essential for life. As they become active in their communities, they begin to understand that they are part of an interconnected system, where every action has an echo and every gesture of kindness reverberates beyond what we can see. The connection with the whole reminds us that, although we are unique individuals, we are all inter-woven in a rich and complex tapestry called life.

In short, by cultivating a sense of purpose in children and encouraging them to connect with the whole, we are laying the groundwork for a future where empathy, responsibility, and collective action prevail. As the writer Antoine de Saint-Exupéry said: "The true discovery does not consist in seeking new landscapes but in having new eyes." May we look at the world with these new eyes and inspire future generations to do the same.

THE EXTRAORDINARY POWER
WITHIN US

Since ancient times, humanity has been faced with a fundamental question: What is, in fact, the power that resides within us? The answer, although complex, can be summarized in one word: creation. "Creation is the purest expression of human freedom," said the renowned philosopher Jean-Paul Sartre. Understanding and embracing this creative power is a journey that we all must undertake, and it begins in childhood.

The power to create manifests in various forms, not limited only to the arts. It permeates all aspects of everyday life: in the way we interact, how we love, and how we challenge ourselves to evolve. Every action we take and every word we utter has the potential to shape our reality and influence those around us. As Mahatma Gandhi said, "You must be the change you wish to see in the world." This quote not only inspires but also reminds us of the responsibility we have to use our creative power to promote positive transformations.

For children, the discovery of this power is an essential process. From the moment they learn to draw until they start formulating their own ideas and opinions, it is crucial that they are encouraged to express themselves. Creativity is the foundation upon which we build our identities; it is the spark that ignites the flame of self-confidence and autonomy. "Creativity is intelligence having fun," said Albert Einstein, emphasizing the importance of viewing the act of creation as play, an exploration. Thus, by cultivating creative expression in children, we are not only nourishing their souls but also laying the foundation for future leaders and innovators.

In a world that often values conformity and obedience, it is vital that educators and parents recognize the importance of nurturing the creative potential of children. This can be done through artistic activities such as painting and writing, but also through science and technology. Stimulating critical thinking and problem-solving is equally essential. As the writer and educator Ken Robinson says, "Creativity now is as important in education as literacy, and we should treat it with the same status." By integrating creativity into learning, we are equipping children with the necessary tools to navigate and transform the world.

Moreover, it is important to remember that the power to create is not limited to the production of something new but also involves the ability to transform what already exists. Innovation often arises from reinterpretation and adaptation. The famous inventor Thomas Edison once stated, "Many of life's failures are people who did not realize how close they were to success when they gave up." This statement teaches us that failure is just a part of the creative process, an opportunity to learn and grow. Therefore, by teaching children to embrace failure as a learning opportunity, we are giving them the freedom to explore without fear.

As we move towards an increasingly complex and interconnected future, the extraordinary power that resides within each of us becomes even more critical. The ability to create, to imagine a different world, and to work collectively towards that ideal is what will allow us to face the looming global challenges. "We do not inherit the earth from our ancestors; we borrow it from our children," said the wise indigenous proverb. This vision reminds us of the importance of building a sustainable and creative legacy for future generations.

In summary, the power that we all possess is extraordinary. It is a tool that, when used wisely, can transform not only our lives but society as a whole. Encouraging creativity, valuing individual expression, and having the courage to dream are essential for us to create a better world together. As the poet Rainer Maria Rilke said, "Creation is eternal. And what is created is always new."

The power that we all possess is, in essence, the power to

create. To create not only in the artistic sense but also in the way we live, love, and interact with the world. Each of us has the capacity to influence others, to transform ideas into actions, and to generate significant changes. It is essential that from a young age, children learn about the strength of their voices and actions. Encouraging creative expression in all its forms—whether through music, dance, writing, or sciences—is fundamental for each individual to recognize their potential. Therefore, let us, with our talents and visions, contribute to this ongoing creation, recognizing the extraordinary power within and around us. May each of us become an agent of change, willing to explore new ideas and challenge the status quo. By embracing creativity and innovation in all their forms, we not only elevate our own lives but also inspire those around us to do the same. Together, we can build a future where individual expression and collective collaboration go hand in hand, where everyone's voices are heard and celebrated. Thus, by cultivating this power in our hearts and minds, we leave a legacy of hope and transformation, a testament that the extraordinary is not just a distant dream, but a reality we can create, day by day, with each action, each word, and each act of love.

OVERCOMING OBSTACLES

The journey of self-discovery is a path filled with challenges and learning experiences. From the first steps to adolescence, children navigate a world that often seems full of obstacles. Social pressures, family expectations, and self-criticism are just some of the barriers that can appear along the way. The question that arises, then, is: how can we prepare future generations to face these adversities in a healthy and constructive way?

One of the keys to this preparation is creating a supportive environment. In a world that often values perfection, it is crucial for children to learn early on that vulnerability is not a sign of weakness, but rather a powerful form of human connection. Brené Brown, a renowned researcher on vulnerability, states: "Vulnerability is the birthplace of innovation, creativity, and change." By encouraging children to express their fears and insecurities openly, we are cultivating a space where they can feel safe to explore their emotions and, consequently, grow.

Moreover, it is essential for mistakes to be seen as learning opportunities rather than failures. The culture of fear surrounding making mistakes can stifle creativity and the courage to try new things. As Thomas Edison said: "I have not failed. I've just found 10,000 ways that won't work." This mindset should be incorporated from the early years of schooling. By creating a school environment that values learning from mistakes, we can help children develop a natural resilience that will accompany them throughout life.

The implementation of workshops on emotional intelligence and resilience in schools can be an effective way to equip young people with the necessary tools to deal with life's ups and downs. These workshops can teach skills such as stress management, empathy, and assertive communication. Emotional intelligence, in particular, is a vital skill that allows individuals to recognize and manage their own emotions and those of others. Daniel Goleman, author of the book *Emotional Intelligence,* highlights that "emotional intelligence is the ability to recognize our own feelings and those of others, to motivate ourselves, and to manage emotions well in ourselves and in our relationships."

However, the responsibility does not fall solely on educational institutions. Parents and caregivers also play a crucial role in this process. Creating a home where emotions are openly discussed and where every mistake is an opportunity for growth can make a significant difference in how children perceive the world around them. The Greek philosopher Aristotle said: "Education is the best provision for old age." And indeed, preparing children for life is not just a matter of academic knowledge but of teaching them to navigate the emotional and social complexities they will encounter along the way.

Finally, it is vital that children see examples of resilience in action, both at home and in society. Stories of overcoming—whether through biographies, literature, or even examples of public figures who have faced adversity—can serve as a source of inspiration. When young people see that others have faced challenges and overcome them, it gives them hope and motivation to move forward, even when the road becomes steep.

Overcoming obstacles is an intrinsic part of the human condition. By creating an environment that values vulnerability, teaches the value of mistakes, and promotes emotional intelligence, we can prepare future generations not just to survive, but to thrive amid adversities. After all, as the famous author Maya Angelou said: "You may encounter many defeats, but you must not be defeated." And it is this mindset that we must cultivate in every child so that they become the architects of their own lives, capable of facing any challenge that life presents to them.

THE IMPORTANCE OF DIVERSITY

In the vast mosaic of humanity, diversity is the paint that colors our collective experience. In such a diverse world, it is vital that everyone learns to value and respect differences. As Maya Angelou said, "Diversity is the one thing we all have in common." This statement reminds us that, despite our different backgrounds, cultures, and beliefs, we all share the same humanity. It is essential that we understand that diversity is not just something to be tolerated but a richness that enriches our lives and broadens our understanding of what it means to be human.

Education plays a crucial role in promoting diversity and inclusion. By incorporating cultural diversity education into school curricula, we can open the minds of young people, allowing them to see the world through different lenses. This not only enriches their knowledge but also helps them develop empathy and connect with others more deeply. The philosopher and educator Paulo Freire argued that "education is an act of love, and therefore, an act of courage." In this context, educating about diversity is an act of courage, challenging prejudices and promoting a more just and equal society.

Diversity is not limited only to visible aspects such as race or ethnicity. It encompasses a wide range of characteristics, including gender, sexual orientation, age, physical and mental abilities, among others. Including all these voices is essential to building an environment where everyone feels valued and respected. As civil rights activist Nelson Mandela declared, "No one is born hating another person because of the color of his skin, his background, or his religion." This teaches us that prejudice is learned, and therefore, it can be unlearned through education and awareness.

When young people are exposed to different cultures, traditions, and ways of life, they learn to appreciate the beauty of diversity. This awareness can be promoted through interactive activities such as cultural exchanges, diversity festivals, and research projects that encourage the exploration of different perspectives. The writer Chimamanda Ngozi Adichie, in her famous speech "The Danger of a Single Story," warns about the importance of listening to multiple stories: "The single story creates stereotypes, and the problem with stereotypes is not that they are untrue, but that they are incomplete." Therefore, by exposing young people to a variety of narratives, we help combat stereotypes and foster a richer and more complex understanding of the world.

Diversity is also a driver of innovation and creativity. When different ideas and experiences meet, new solutions and approaches to complex problems emerge. The famous quote by Steve Jobs, "Creativity is just connecting things," reminds us that the best innovations often emerge at the intersection of different cultures and perspectives. In a globalized scenario, where the challenges faced by humanity are increasingly interconnected, the ability to collaborate in a diverse environment is essential for progress.

Furthermore, promoting diversity in schools and communities plays a crucial role in preparing young people for a connected world. As the boundaries between countries and cultures become increasingly blurred, the ability to work and relate with people from different backgrounds becomes an indispensable skill. Former U.S. President Barack Obama emphasized, "Change will not come if we wait for someone else or another time. We are the ones we've been waiting for." This call to action encourages us to become advocates of diversity, not just in our words, but in our daily actions.

Ultimately, diversity is an opportunity, not an obstacle. As a society, we must embrace this richness and learn to see differences as a source of strength. The renowned activist and writer Audre Lorde said, "I am not free while any other woman is unfree." This perspective reminds us that the struggle for diversity and inclusion is a collective struggle, a battle we must face together.

Thus, by promoting education about diversity in schools and communities, we are not only preparing young people to be more conscious global citizens, but also building a future where empathy, respect, and inclusion are the norms. May we, therefore, value and celebrate the differences that make us unique, and in doing so, discover the beauty and strength that emerge from our shared diversity. By cultivating an environment where everyone feels welcome and respected, we are not only promoting social justice but also building a brighter and more harmonious future. A future where empathy and understanding guide our interactions, and where every voice, regardless of its origin, is heard and valued. Together, we can transform the world into a space where diversity is not only recognized but celebrated, paving the way for a tomorrow that respects and honors the rich tapestry of human experience.

In such a diverse world, it is vital that everyone learns to value and respect differences. Diversity is a richness that enriches our lives and broadens our understanding of what it means to be human. Incorporating education about cultural diversity and inclusion into school curricula can open young minds, allowing them to see the world through different lenses and thus connect with others more deeply.

THE ESSENCE OF DUALITY

Duality is a fundamental principle that permeates human existence and the cosmos. Since ancient times, philosophers, spiritualists, and scientists have explored the nature of this duality, realizing that without the presence of opposites, life as we know it would not exist. As the Greek philosopher Heraclitus said, "Struggle is the father of all things." This struggle, or tension, between opposites is what enables us to understand and experience reality.

Duality manifests in various aspects of life. Light and darkness, love and hate, life and death, joy and sadness are just a few examples of how these opposites interact and complement each other. Light, for instance, is only perceived in contrast with darkness. The artist and writer Anaïs Nin stated, "We don't see things as they are; we see them as we are." This quote reminds us that our perception is shaped by the internal and external dualities that reside within us. The way we interpret our experiences depends on how we balance and reconcile these opposites.

In Eastern philosophy, particularly in Taoism, this idea is encapsulated in the concept of Yin and Yang. Yin is often associated with darkness, passivity, and femininity, while Yang represents light, activity, and masculinity. Together, they form a dynamic and interdependent cycle, where each part contains the seed of the other. As Lao Tzu, the author of the Tao Te Ching, said, "When you accept everything, everything becomes possible." This acceptance is not resignation but a deep understanding that duality is an intrinsic part of life.

Duality is also reflected in human emotions. Every feeling, no matter how positive, can contain the seed of its counterpart. For example, love can transform into jealousy or possessiveness, while joy can give way to sadness in times of loss. The renowned psychologist Carl Jung stated, "The shadow is not just evil; the shadow is also the unrecognized part of the self." Recognizing and integrating these shadowy parts is essential for personal growth and building an authentic life. By accepting the duality within us, we can begin to free ourselves from the limitations it imposes.

Duality is not limited to the individual but also extends to society. Divisions between groups, social classes, races, and ideologies are clear examples of how duality permeates human interactions. The leader and activist Martin Luther King Jr. highlighted this reality by stating, "Injustice anywhere is a threat to justice everywhere." This quote emphasizes the importance of recognizing that all actions and decisions have repercussions that transcend the individual. The fight for equality and justice is, in essence, a call to transcend the duality that separates us and unite in a common purpose.

As we navigate the complexities of duality, it is crucial to remember that while opposites may seem antagonistic, they are also interdependent. Life is a cycle of transformation, where death is necessary for rebirth, and pain often precedes healing. The philosopher Friedrich Nietzsche captured this idea by saying, "What does not kill me makes me stronger." This perspective allows us to understand that the challenges and difficulties we face are opportunities for growth and learning.

Moreover, duality offers us a rich tapestry of experiences. Each emotion, each challenge, and each joy brings with it a valuable lesson. The writer and activist Maya Angelou expressed this wisdom by stating, "I've learned that people will forget what you said, people will forget what you did, but people will never forget how you made them feel." This quote reminds us that, ultimately, how we navigate duality determines the relationships we build and the impact we have on others.

As we reflect on the essence of duality, we are invited to recognize that we need not fear opposites, but rather embrace them. True wisdom lies in the ability to see beyond appearances and understand that, ultimately, all opposites are parts of a greater whole. As the Greek philosopher Plato said, "The greatest mistake we can make is to think that we are separated." This separation is an illusion that prevents us from perceiving the interconnectedness of all things.

Therefore, as we explore the essence of duality, we are challenged to cultivate compassion and empathy, both towards ourselves and others. Recognizing that each of us carries our own struggles and triumphs allows us to build bridges instead of walls. True transformation happens when we choose to embrace the complexity of life, recognizing that duality is not an obstacle to be overcome, but an essential part of our journey. By accepting and integrating these opposites, we can become more complete human beings, capable of living with authenticity and love. Ultimately, the essence of duality invites us to dance with life, to respect its nuances, and to find beauty in the interconnectedness of all things, allowing us to expand our consciousness and create a world where unity and diversity coexist in harmony.

"We are spiritual beings having a physical experience." — **Pierre Teilhard de Chardin**

In a world where reality is often limited to the tangible, to what we can see, touch, and measure, the phrase "We are spiritual beings having a physical experience" emerges as an invitation to deep reflection and the exploration of invisible layers of human existence. What does it really mean to be a spiritual being? How does this ethereal essence interact with flesh, the senses, and the limitations of the body? This chapter proposes to unravel the rich tapestry that makes up the relationship between spirit and matter, challenging the conventional perception that often imprisons us in a monolithic view of life.

Let us imagine, for a moment, that we are temporary travelers in a vast and wonderful universe. Our souls, before incarnating, are like seeds scattered to the wind, each carrying the potential to transform into something beautiful and unique. As we enter our physical bodies, we are gifted with a unique sensory experience — the ability to feel, to touch, to love, and to learn. However, this experience, although rich and multifaceted, can often lead us away from our true essence. We get lost in routines, obligations, and social expectations, forgetting that we are, above all, beings of light and consciousness.

One of the greatest challenges on this journey is the tendency to identify exclusively with the physical form. Society, with its conventions and norms, often encourages us to measure our worth and success through material achievements. However, this perspective is limited and can lead to an identity crisis. The spirit, which is intrinsically free and expansive, feels imprisoned in a body that, by its nature, is ephemeral. The disconnection between being and having generates an existential void that many seek to fill with possessions, status, or external validation.

To understand this duality, we can look to spiritual and

philosophical traditions that speak to us about the unity between body and spirit. The concept of "everything is one" invites us to realize that, even while living in a physical world, we are all intertwined in a web of energy and consciousness. This implies that our actions, thoughts, and emotions not only affect us but reverberate in the universe around us. As spiritual beings, each interaction we have is an opportunity for growth and learning, not just for ourselves but for the collective.

However, it is essential to recognize the obstacles that arise on this journey of self-discovery. Social pressure, fear of the unknown, and resistance to change can create significant barriers. Often, we feel alone in this quest, as if we are the only ones questioning the nature of reality. Here, creativity becomes a powerful tool. Through art, music, writing, and personal expression, we can explore and share our spiritual experiences in ways that resonate with others. These creations not only allow us to express our individuality but also connect us to a broader community of seekers.

Practically, how can we fully live this duality of being spiritual beings in a physical reality? The answer can be found in daily practices that nourish both body and spirit. Meditation, for example, offers a sacred space to quiet the mind and listen to the inner voice. By cultivating mindfulness, we can rediscover the presence of the spirit that resides within us, allowing this light to guide our actions in the physical world. Similarly, practices such as dance, yoga, or even walking in nature help us integrate the experience of the body with the essence of the spirit, promoting a state of harmony and balance.

Moreover, authentic relationships are fundamental on this journey. By surrounding ourselves with people who share a similar vision or who are open to spiritual exploration, we create an environment conducive to mutual growth. The stories we exchange, the experiences we live together, and the challenges we overcome become part of a great spiritual mosaic that enriches the lives of all involved. Human connection, when lived with presence and empathy, is one of the purest forms of experiencing the reality of being spiritual beings in a physical body.

Finally, when looking at the phrase "We are spiritual beings having a physical experience," we are invited to reimagine our existence. We are not mere bodies wandering in a material world; we are vibrant souls, each with its own journey, contributing to the grand tapestry of the universe. Each of us carries a unique spark of divine consciousness, and by connecting with this essence, we begin to perceive that our physical life is a precious opportunity to learn, grow, and express this light.

In this context, the concept of purpose gains a new dimension. It's not just about achieving material goals or fulfilling social roles, but understanding that each action, each thought, and each emotion is a contribution to the whole. Each challenge faced is a lesson that drives us to evolve, and each moment of joy is a celebration of life and the experience of being human. By accepting that we are spiritual beings, we can begin to see our daily interactions as opportunities to manifest the love, compassion, and wisdom that dwell within us.

As we delve deeper into this journey of self-discovery, the possibility arises for us to transcend the duality between body and spirit. Mindfulness practices, gratitude, and compassion become not just tools but a way of life. When we learn to live in the present, honoring each moment as sacred, our perception expands, allowing us to see beyond the limitations of physical form. We begin to perceive that we are all interconnected, that the barriers we often construct are illusory, and that, deep down, we are all in search of the same universal truths.

Thus, by embracing this broader vision, life transforms into a cosmic dance where each of us is both the dancer and the music. The creation of art, spiritual practice, and authentic relationships all interlace into a symphony of experiences that enrich not only our lives but also the fabric of humanity. The simple act of living then becomes an act of conscious creation, where each of us has the ability to leave an indelible mark on the world, inspiring others to awaken to their own spiritual reality.

In this way, the phrase "We are spiritual beings having a physical experience" invites us to a continuous reflection on who we are and how we choose to live. It challenges us to look beyond the surface, to explore the mysteries of our own existence, and to open up to the greatness of what it means to be human. Thus, by becoming aware of this truth, we can become agents of change, not only in our lives but in the world around us. The spiritual journey then becomes a collective journey, where each step taken toward our essence brings us closer to unity, peace, and universal love.

Thus, as we continue to tread this path, we can remember that the physical experience is a gift, an opportunity to manifest the light that we are. And, at the end of our journey, we can look back and realize that, despite the difficulties and challenges, we lived fully as spiritual beings, leaving a legacy of love, compassion, and connection that transcends time and space. It is in this profound realization that we find the true meaning of life: not just to exist, but to live with purpose, authenticity, and a deep reverence for the beauty of being.

THE ORIGIN OF FEARS AND THE UNITY OF CONSCIOUSNESS

"Fear is not the absence of courage, but the triumph of fear over courage." — **Nelson Mandela**

Since the dawn of humanity, fears have been a driving force in the human experience. They emerge as shadows cast over our consciousness, shaping not only our individual actions but also the social dynamics that surround us. To understand the origin of fears, it is essential to return to the core of our existence: the idea that we all share a single consciousness, an essence that transcends the limitations of the physical body and time.

Fears can be seen as adaptive responses developed over the course of evolution to ensure survival. Our ancestors, in a world full of dangers, learned to respond to threats quickly and instinctively. This survival instinct, although vital in ancient times, also generated a series of fears that are perpetuated through generations. Over time, these instinctive responses have become part of the collective narrative of humanity, rooted in our experiences and in the stories we tell each other.

The origin of fears is, therefore, multifaceted. They can originate from traumatic personal experiences, but they are also influenced by cultural and social factors. Society, in its quest for control and security, often fuels fears that are not intrinsically ours but are imposed on us. Fears such as rejection, failure, and inadequacy intertwine with behavioral patterns and social expectations, creating a complex web that traps us in cycles of anxiety and insecurity.

However, it is essential to recognize that these fears are, in essence, illusions of the human mind. The mind, in its relentless pursuit of control and predictability, often creates catastrophic scenarios that do not correspond to reality. This illusion feeds on the separation we perceive in our daily lives. The belief that we are isolated individuals, disconnected from each other and the universe, is one of the main sources of fear. When we forget that we are all part of a single consciousness, we begin to see the world as a hostile place, where survival becomes the top priority.

The reality, however, is much more subtle and interconnected. Quantum physics and spiritual philosophies teach us that everything is interconnected. Every thought, every emotion, and every action resonates in the fabric of reality, affecting not only ourselves but everyone around us. When we recognize our connection, we begin to dissipate the shadows that fears cast over our perception. The unity of consciousness invites us to see that what we fear in others also resides within us. By confronting our fears, we not only free ourselves but also those around us.

The journey of facing fears is, therefore, an internal voyage. By looking inward, we can begin to dismantle the beliefs that uphold our fears. Practices of self-reflection, meditation, and mindfulness offer us tools to observe our thoughts without identifying with them. This observation allows us to realize that fears are often just temporary thoughts that do not define who we are. When we distance ourselves from the narrative the mind creates, we begin to see life from a new perspective — one where courage and compassion can flourish.

Humanity, as one consciousness, has the ability to transcend its collective fears. When an individual chooses to embrace vulnerability and authenticity, it resonates beyond themselves, creating a ripple effect that can inspire others to do the same. The courage of a single heart can ignite the flame of change in many. By recognizing that we are all interconnected, we can transform fear into love, separation into unity.

Moreover, it is vital to remember that everything we experience is temporary. The external circumstances, the emotions, and even the fears we feel are ephemeral. Life, in its essence, is a constant flow of experiences and transitions.

When we learn to see fear as part of the journey, rather than an insurmountable obstacle, we begin to create space for transformation. Each confronted fear becomes an opportunity for growth and evolution, allowing us to discover deeper layers of who we truly are.

As we explore the origin of fears and their influence on us and on humanity, we are invited to recognize the great tapestry of life. Each of us is a unique thread, but together, we form a magnificent and complex pattern that reveals the beauty of our interconnection. This tapestry of life reminds us that, by facing our fears, we are not only freeing ourselves but also contributing to collective healing.

When an individual rises and decides to break the chains of fear, they are, in essence, illuminating the path for others who are still trapped in darkness. This light is not just an individual force but a vibration that echoes throughout humanity.

The transformation of fear into love begins with a conscious choice: the choice to see the world through the lens of compassion. When we start to see ourselves as part of a whole, our daily interactions become opportunities for empathy and understanding. Each encounter becomes a reflection of our own journey, and what we see in others is often a reflection of what we have yet to face in ourselves. This realization is powerful, as it offers us the chance to learn and grow together.

It is essential to cultivate practices that nurture this new perspective. Meditation, for example, allows us to quiet the mind and connect with the essence of our being. Through practice, we can observe our fears without judgment, allowing them to come and go like passing clouds in a vast sky. This practice of acceptance is fundamental, as it teaches us that we do not need to identify with our fears; instead, we can see them as part of our growth.

The art of storytelling — both ours and others' — plays a crucial role in demystifying fears. By sharing our experiences, we create a safe space for others to do the same. Stories of overcoming, vulnerability, and connection have the power to bring people together, showing that we are not alone in our struggles. Through narrative, we can transform our personal fears into something collective, a testimony to human resilience that echoes through generations.

The unity of consciousness teaches us that although fears are a natural part of the human experience, they do not need to define our destiny. Instead, we can choose courage, authenticity, and love as our guides. This choice is not only a personal transformation but a movement that reverberates throughout humanity, inspiring others to free themselves from their own chains.

True freedom is found in the acceptance that we are all part of the same fabric of existence. By acknowledging and facing our fears, we not only free ourselves but also contribute to a world where empathy and compassion prevail. Thus, each of our journeys intertwines, creating a symphony of experiences where each note, each fear overcome, and each act of love becomes part of a greater harmony.

Therefore, as we look to the future, we are guided by the hope that together we can transform our fears into a powerful drive for change. May we unite with the courage to be vulnerable, the strength to be authentic, and the determination to build a world where the unity of consciousness is celebrated. Because in the end, we are all one—a single consciousness navigating the complexities of life in search of meaning, connection, and love.

As we advance on this journey of transformation, it is essential to recognize that change begins within us. The first step is self-reflection, an invitation to look within and confront our own fears and insecurities. This introspection allows us to understand the roots of our feelings and behaviors. By doing so, we begin to dismantle the barriers we have built over time, allowing the light of understanding and compassion to enter our hearts.

The practice of gratitude also plays a vital role in this process. By focusing on the things we are grateful for, we change our perspective and begin to see the world through a more positive lens. Gratitude helps us value the small daily victories and recognize the beauty that surrounds us, even in difficult times. This shift in focus allows us to cultivate a mindset of abundance, where fear and scarcity lose their grip on us.

Moreover, connection with others is essential. In a world often marked by division and isolation, finding communities that share our values and aspirations can be a balm for the soul. These communities offer us support, understanding, and a safe space to express our vulnerabilities. By coming together, we create a network of love and support that allows us to face our fears collectively, strengthening our resilience and determination.

Education is also a powerful tool in transforming fear into love. By educating ourselves about the experiences and challenges of others, we are able to cultivate empathy and understanding. Education teaches us that the differences that often separate us are, in fact, opportunities to learn and grow. When we open ourselves to listen and understand others' stories, we begin to break down the prejudices that fuel fear and distrust.

It is equally important to remember that transformation does not happen overnight. It is a continuous process filled with ups and downs. There will be moments when fears resurface, challenging our courage and determination. However, it is in these moments that we must remember that vulnerability is a strength, not a weakness. By accepting our fears as part of the journey, we can learn to dance with them instead of fighting against them. This dance, full of awareness and acceptance, empowers us to move forward with a lighter and more open heart.

As we strive on the mission to transform fear into love, we must also remember to celebrate small victories. Each step taken toward courage and authenticity deserves to be recognized and celebrated. These celebrations not only motivate us to continue but also inspire those around us to join us on this path of transformation. When we share our stories of overcoming and moments of joy that arise along the journey, we create a space of hope and inspiration that can encourage others to do the same.

It is vital that, as we pursue this personal and collective transformation, we maintain a vision of a more enlightened future—a future where love and understanding are the driving forces of our actions, a future where everyone's voices are heard and respected, and where empathy becomes the norm rather than the exception. This vision is not just a dream but a real possibility that we can achieve together, one step at a time.

Therefore, as we look to the horizon, may we commit to living by the principles of compassion, empathy, and unconditional love. May we be beacons of hope in a world that often seems dark, and may each of us become an agent of change, willing to transform fear into love and create a brighter future for all. Together, we can weave a new narrative, a story of unity, strength, and resilience, where each of us plays a crucial role in building a better world.

THE STAGE OF LIFE

We all inhabit a living, pulsating, and constantly changing scenario. Life is not a static canvas; it is an ongoing film where each act unfolds before our eyes. The way each of us plays our part on this vast stage determines not only our experience but also that of the people around us. As the Greek philosopher Heraclitus once said, "Nothing is permanent except change." This incessant change invites us to reflect on the power we hold in our hands.

Our attitudes and emotions are the tools with which we paint our reality. What we think, feel, and say not only shapes our personal experience but also reverberates in the lives of those around us. It is an echo that resonates, affecting the emotional environment of everyone.

Imagine the scene: an actor who skillfully uses his voice and expressions to evoke the audience's empathy. Just like in theater, we are all protagonists of our narratives. What matters is not only what happens to us but how we choose to react to it.

"What you do makes a difference, and you have to decide what kind of difference you want to make," said Jane Goodall. This choice is the core of our experience. We are not mere supporting actors in other people's stories; we are the authors of our lives. Regardless of external expectations or opinions, each of us carries the responsibility to perform our role with authenticity. Even if others' intentions are good, true transformation comes from within.

Within each of us resides immense power—an inexhaustible source of creative energy. This energy is neither distant nor out of our reach; it pulsates within us, ready to be accessed. However, we often allow the information we receive throughout our lives to condition and limit us. Most of these beliefs are not the result of our own creation but a web of ideas and concepts perpetuated from generation to generation.

However, when we connect to this cosmic energy that created us, we begin to dismantle the barriers imposed on us. We can rewrite the narrative of our lives, transform what troubles us, and challenge the limitations we were taught. As Albert Einstein said, "The mind that opens to a new idea never returns to its original size." By opening our minds to new possibilities, we can transcend limitations and create rich and meaningful experiences.

Therefore, remember that life is an art, and you are the artist. The palette of colors, emotions, and experiences is in your hands. By taking control of your story, you not only transform yourself but also inspire others to do the same. The stage of life is vast and full of opportunities; it's time to shine and leave your indelible mark on this masterpiece called existence.

THE POWER OF A SIMPLE SMILE

A genuine smile carries with it a transformative power that we often underestimate. This simple yet profound expression transcends cultural and linguistic barriers, being a universal language that communicates joy, kindness, and the essence of human connection. As the famous writer and activist Maya Angelou said, "People will forget what you said, people will forget what you did, but people will never forget how you made them feel." A genuine smile is a powerful way to make others feel valued and loved.

First and foremost, a genuine smile has the power to light up someone's day. When we authentically smile at another person, we send a clear message that we care. This simple gesture can be like a ray of sunshine piercing through a cloudy day, bringing hope and renewal. The writer Helen Keller once said, "Nothing can be more meaningful than a smile." Indeed, a smile can instantly change someone's mood, creating a lighter and more positive atmosphere.

Furthermore, the power of a smile extends to the ability to create meaningful connections between people. A smile is an invitation to interaction, showing that we are open to connecting emotionally. This connection can lead to more authentic interactions, strengthen existing relationships, and even give rise to new friendships. The famous philosopher and educator Jean-Paul Sartre stated, "If you understand me, that's good; if you don't understand me, that's a smile." Thus, a genuine smile has the potential to open doors and build bridges between individuals of different backgrounds and perspectives.

The positive impact of a smile also reflects on our mental and emotional health. When we smile, our body releases endorphins, known as the "happiness hormones," which act as natural painkillers and improve our overall well-being. Studies show that smiling can reduce stress, alleviate anxiety, and even improve the immune system. The author and psychology professor Shawn Achor notes that "happiness is not the result of success, but rather the source of it." Therefore, a smile not only brightens someone's day but also reflects on our own happiness and confidence.

And most impressively, a smile is contagious. When we smile at someone, it is highly likely that person will smile back. This chain effect can quickly spread through a community, creating a more positive and welcoming environment. The famous psychologist and philosopher William James said, "Action seems to be a source of emotion." A simple act of kindness, like a smile, can inspire a series of kind acts, showing that kindness is indeed a skill we can cultivate and share.

The value of a genuine smile goes beyond words. It can bring joy, create meaningful connections, promote mental and emotional health, and spread kindness throughout the world. It is a reminder that, even in difficult times, the simplicity of a smile can have a profound impact. Therefore, never underestimate the power of a smile. Next time you meet someone, remember the impact a genuine smile can have and share it generously. After all, as the great Greek philosopher Aristotle said, "Happiness depends upon ourselves." And often, it begins with a simple smile.

The Alchemy of Desire

(mantra) - "My vision is clear and my heart is open. Success and happiness gravitate around me. Obstacles disappear as my intentions strengthen and my desires are effortlessly fulfilled." Louise Hay

The soft light of dawn filtered through the curtains, creating a pattern of dancing shadows on the floor. Sitting on the edge of the bed, Lara closed her eyes and took a deep breath. "My vision is clear and my heart is open. Success and happiness gravitate around me." These words echoed in her mind, like a mantra she had repeated countless times. It was a powerful reminder that what she desired was within reach, if only she had the courage to allow herself.

Inspired by the wisdom of Ralph Waldo Emerson, who said, "What lies behind us and what lies before us are tiny matters compared to what lies within us," Lara reflected on her journey. Every moment of doubt and every obstacle she had faced became an essential part of who she was. The path had not been easy, but each challenge shaped her, taught her, and prepared her for what was to come.

As she rose and headed to the window, the city slowly awoke. The sounds of urban life mixed with the birdsong, and Lara knew the day was full of possibilities. She remembered the words of Maya Angelou: "You can't control all the events that happen to you, but you can decide not to be reduced by them." And so, she decided that today would be different. Today, she would not let fears and insecurities cloud her vision.

With determination, Lara began to write in her journal. "Obstacles disappear as my intentions strengthen." That was her mantra for the day. As she put pen to paper, she allowed herself to dream big. What would her goals be? What truly made her happy? She began listing her intentions, from small daily achievements to big life dreams.

"My desires are effortlessly fulfilled." This statement seemed magical, but Lara knew the true magic was in action. For each desire, she mapped out a plan. What steps would be necessary? What resources would she need to gather? The paper filled with ideas and strategies, and as she wrote, she felt the vibrant energy of the universe aligning with her.

Later, when meeting with friends, Lara shared her new perspective. "Success is not just what you achieve in life, but what you inspire others to do." Eleanor Roosevelt's words echoed in her mind, and looking at her friends, she realized they were a source of mutual support. Together, they discussed their aspirations, encouraging each other to dream and act.

That night, after a day full of reflection and connection, Lara sat down to meditate. She visualized her desires, feeling the emotion of having already realized them. With each breath, she remembered the words of Paulo Coelho: "When you want something, all the universe conspires in helping you to achieve it." It was a reminder that she was not alone in her journey; the universe was by her side.

Lara fell asleep with a smile on her lips, knowing that tomorrow would bring new opportunities and that, with a clear vision and an open heart, she could turn her dreams into reality.

THE RESPONSIBILITY OF CONSCIOUSNESS

In the vast tapestry of human history, few moments are as crucial as those when indifference settles in people's hearts. Martin Luther King Jr. reminds us that the real danger does not only lie in the oppression exercised by those in power but in the silent apathy of those who could make a difference —the "good" people. This indifference is a poison that infiltrates the depths of society, suffocating hope and perpetuating injustice. If we are not vigilant, this apathy can turn into an abyss, where suffering becomes the norm and compassion an exception.

What does it mean to be "good" in a world full of inequalities and injustices? The answer is not simple. However, Pythagoras offers us a profound reflection by stating that "while laws are necessary for men, they are not sufficient to guarantee freedom." Laws, as just as they may be, often fail to address the nuances of human morality and social responsibility. They can establish limits, but they do not have the power to touch the hearts and minds of people. True freedom is not found in following rules, but in acting consciously and ethically.

This collective consciousness is what separates us from an endless cycle of destruction and pain. Pythagoras, in his wisdom, also warns us: "As long as man continues to be the ruthless destroyer of lower living beings, he will never know health or peace." This statement echoes in our days, where rampant exploitation of nature and disregard for the lives of other species are evident. What are we sowing in our world? If we continue to cultivate violence, greed, and indifference, we will inevitably harvest a future full of pain and sadness.

The interconnectedness of all forms of life is a concept that we often forget. The health of our planet and its creatures is intrinsically linked to our own health. When we harm the earth, pollute rivers, exterminate species, and ignore the suffering of others, we are, in fact, digging our own grave. "He who sows the seeds of murder and pain will not reap joy and love." This is a truth that transcends time and space, a lesson that we all need to internalize.

Therefore, the responsibility lies with each of us. What can we do to combat indifference? How can we free ourselves from the shackles of laws that do not promote true freedom? The answer is in cultivating an active consciousness. It is not just about acting in moments of crisis, but developing a daily commitment to justice, compassion, and empathy.

This means listening to silenced voices, amplifying the cries for help that echo on the margins of society, and recognizing that every act of kindness, no matter how small, can have a profound impact. It means educating ourselves and others, challenging the norms that perpetuate inequality and pain. It means fighting against the indifference that, like a shadow, stretches across our lives.

In a world that often seems to be falling apart, hope still shines. Change begins when we decide not to be passive spectators but active protagonists in the quest for a more just and balanced world. Each of us has the power to transform reality, to sow love and compassion, and to cultivate a future in which everyone can flourish.

As we reflect on the words of Martin Luther King, Pythagoras, and so many others, we are called to act. History watches us, and future generations will depend on our choices. May we, then, embrace the responsibility that comes with consciousness and work together to create a world where indifference has no place, where freedom is a right for all, and where peace and health can finally be established.

Thank you for embarking on this journey with me. May we continue to explore the power of the written word and the magic it brings. Until the next adventure!

With gratitude,

Miguel Almeida

In the silence of your breathing, listen to your heart.

That's where your true essence lives.

Leave a footprint on the world that cannot be erased.

The best of me today for a better world.

Let your heart speak - Listen in silence.